IMAGES
of America

PORTLAND
FIRE & RESCUE

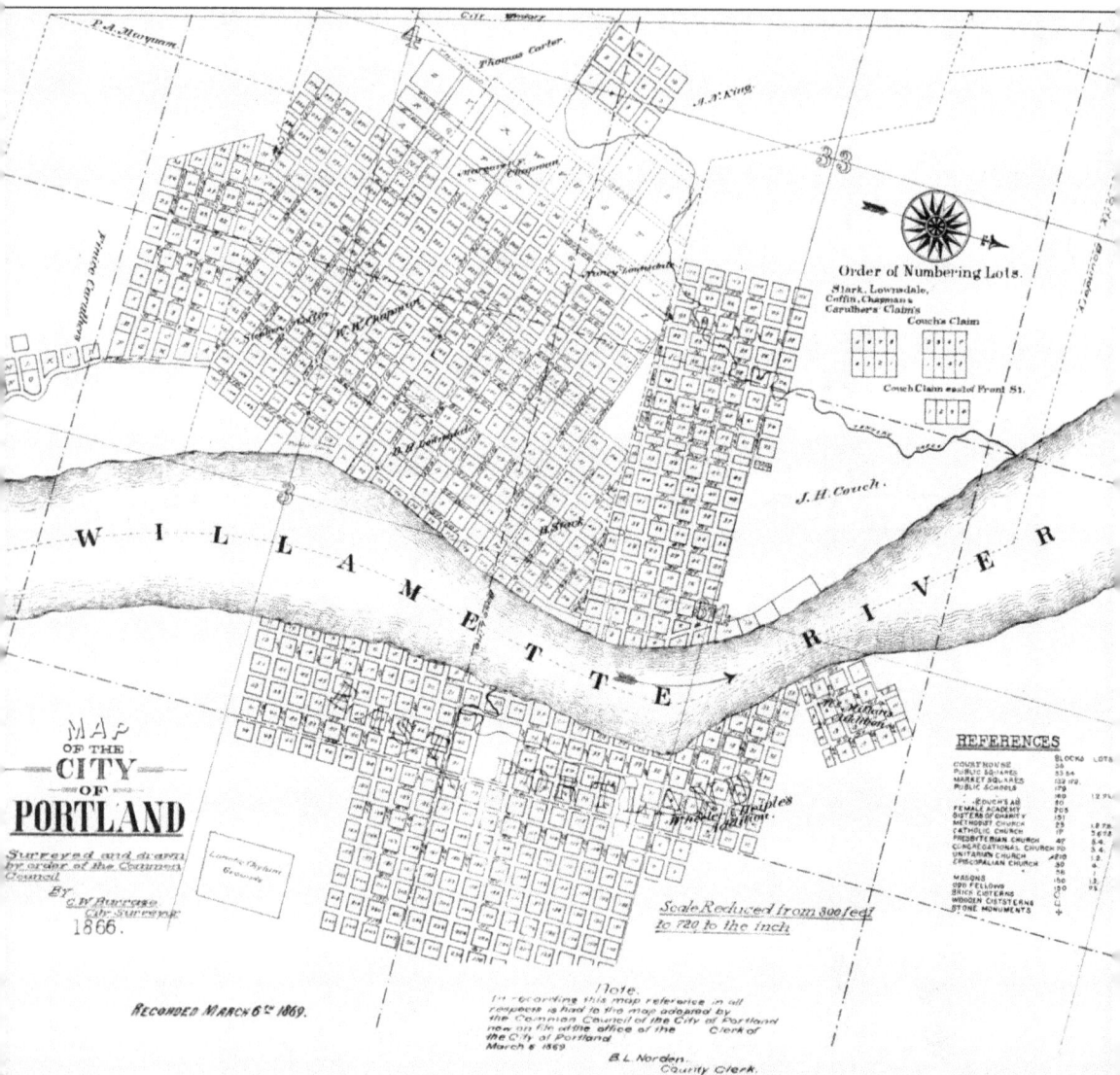

MAP OF PORTLAND, OREGON, 1866. This map was created by city surveyor C. W. Burrage after the Portland City Council ordered an accurate map of the city be produced.

ON THE COVER: STATION NO. 9, 1908. Capt. William Hansen (right on hose wagon) and his crew pose in front of their fire station located at Southeast Thirty-fifth Avenue and Belmont Street. The engine (right) is a fifth-class Amoskeag. This wooden structure was replaced by a brick building at the same location in 1912. Today, the retired station houses Portland Fire & Rescue's Safety Learning Center & Fire Museum. (City of Portland Archives.)

IMAGES
of America

PORTLAND
FIRE & RESCUE

Brian K. Johnson and Don Porth

ARCADIA
PUBLISHING

Published by Arcadia Publishing
Charleston SC, Chicago IL, Portsmouth NH, San Francisco CA

Library of Congress Catalog Card Number: 2006939695

For all general information contact Arcadia Publishing at:
Telephone 843-853-2070
Faxe 843-853-0044
E-mail sales@arcadiapublishing.com
For customer service and orders:
Toll-Free 1-888-313-2665

Visit us on the Internet at www.arcadiapublishing.com

This book is dedicated to the memory of Jefferson D. Morris. "Fireman Jeff" joined the Portland Fire Bureau in 1943 at the age of 15. In 1974, Jeff died of cancer at the age of 46. He was serving as a battalion chief at that time. Jeff's devotion to the fire bureau led him to become what one city commissioner called "Portland's best-known city employee."
He spent numerous hours spreading the word of fire safety and fire prevention among Portland's schoolchildren, civic clubs, and through other public meetings. Jeff became the bureau's unofficial "ambassador of goodwill." In 1982, a group of his friends formed the Friends of Jeff Morris committee. Today the Jeff Morris Fire & Life Safety Foundation continues to support Portland Fire & Rescue. The Safety Learning Center & Fire Museum is a living legacy to the vision and passion of Fireman Jeff. It shares the story of the fire service in Portland, allowing citizens to understand the need for emergency services. More importantly, it shares the steps that citizens can take to live more safely.

CONTENTS

ACKNOWLEDGMENTS

This book was made possible through the efforts of hundreds of individuals who have contributed time and materials to the City of Portland over the last few decades. Portland's active and retired firefighters and their families have made donations of historical materials and have spent countless hours identifying and describing the people and activities that those materials document. They have also shared their stories to help enrich these collections and to make this book a much more vibrant example of our fire department's history.

Special mention must be made of retired captain Gale Buchanan, who visited the archives over 50 times and painstakingly reviewed all of the nearly 50 boxes of photographs; Richard Howard, who reviewed the same boxes and identified every motorized apparatus that could be found; all of the Portland Fire Department retirees and "Old Flames" who have made visits to the archives and who have allowed us to take part in their breakfasts and other meetings; and all of those who have made donations of the materials that are part of the book or assisted in bringing it about.

Special thanks also to Norman Gohlston and Donald Nelson for generously sharing images from their collections. Those images help illustrate the early days of the fire department. Donald Nelson must also be acknowledged for lending his expertise in identifying place names and locations in some photographs included in this work. Thanks as well to Leann Arndt and Kerri Creager, who lent their expertise with regard to content analysis.

INTRODUCTION

This book presents the history of Portland Fire & Rescue from 1851 through the 1970s. While much more detail is available than this book will allow, the information offers a compelling look into one of the most unique professions in the world.

Firefighters have served Portland since 1851, when Pioneer Engine Company No. 1 was formed. While Pioneer never came together as an official part of Portland Fire & Rescue's historic tale, it led the way for other volunteer companies, such as Willamette, Multnomah, Columbian, Protection, and Tiger Engine Companies, as well as Vigilance Hook and Ladder. Other fire companies in areas surrounding Portland developed and eventually became part of the Portland Fire Department.

Like most fire departments, Portland's experienced many growing pains through the years. Change was the constant variable that made perfection an elusive goal. Through it all, dedication to service and the citizens of Portland has been the continuing theme.

Today Portland Fire & Rescue continues to meet the changing needs of the City of Portland. The ability to do so rests on a solid foundation of knowledge and on an understanding of the past. Fortunately Portland Fire & Rescue and the City of Portland Archives have saved many documents and artifacts that capture and preserve the past. The Oregon Historical Society has also collected and preserved many important historical items. More importantly, the institutional memory of the many past members of the fire department is the real key to this history.

Except where noted, all of the images and documents that appear in this book come from the City of Portland Archives. These images come mainly from two sources: the fire department's official photographers and donations from past firefighters and others interested in Portland firefighting history. Many of the facts, anecdotes, and quotations come from scrapbooks, textual items, and oral histories from those who collected them throughout the 20th century.

Statement of Cost of Columbian Fire Engine & No 3.

Wm Jeffers & Co. bill of Engine and apparatus	$ 2500.00
Insurance 4%. on $2500 policy 1.25	101.25
Expenses from New York to Pawtucket.	11.80
Frt for Ship David Brown.	203.20
Cartage & Storage at San Francisco	27.66
Exchange on remittance of $1250 = $ Lacy & Tilton	47.25
Do Do 1250 = 2½% from S F Co	31.25
$ Wm Jeffers & Co Interest on $1250. from apl 2 to	
July 2 = 3 months @ 8% pr annum.	25.00
Commission p⁰ for purchase 2½% on $2500 -	62.50
	$ 3009.91
Cr. Amount received from City Treasurer	1500.00
Balance due	1509.91

Portland O. October 17 1860

STATEMENT OF ACCOUNT FOR A JEFFERS HAND-PUMP ENGINE, OCTOBER 1860. Purchased for volunteer company Columbian No. 3, this engine is still owned by the department and is on display in the Safety Learning Center & Fire Museum.

One

VOLUNTEER FIREFIGHTING
IN PORTLAND

The history of Portland's volunteer fire department begins with the founding of Pioneer Engine Company in the spring of 1851, the same year the city was officially incorporated. The city's growth and the conflagration of 1873 brought about changes to the organization of the volunteer companies and gave impetus to the creation of the Portland Paid Fire Department (PPFD) in 1883.

The advent of the PPFD did not bring an end to volunteer firefighting, however. The PPFD replaced the downtown core-area volunteer companies with paid firefighters, but the force was small, and volunteers continued to work side-by-side with the paid department. Volunteer firefighters became even more important with Portland's 1891 consolidation with East Portland and Albina, which more than doubled the size of the service area. Volunteering was a good way to work one's way onto the paid staff, and good teamsters were always valuable assets to a department that was at that point fully powered by horses rather than by hand-drawn apparatus.

In 1904, the Portland Fire Department (PFD) became fully paid, with all temporary firefighters being paid for their services. However, this did not mean an end to volunteerism outside of the official fire department, as outlying areas or neighborhoods that felt underserved still maintained volunteer companies that were supplied hose by the PFD. Most but not all of those companies were gone by the 1930s.

The advent of World War II saw a major resurgence in volunteer firefighting efforts. Auxiliary companies were established to supplement a force that was weakened by the war effort. These volunteers differed from the late-19th-century volunteers in that they were not integrated with the front-line force but made up fully separate companies designated with reserve numbers.

The auxiliary force expanded during the cold war with a full complement of reserve firefighters, including officers and chiefs, comprising seven distinct districts. In 1963, Portland became the first major U.S. city to disaffiliate with the Federal Civil Defense Administration. As a result, the auxiliary department was cut as well, ending Portland's active involvement with volunteer firefighting.

OFFICERS OF PORTLAND'S VOLUNTEER FIRE DEPARTMENT, 1864. During this era, the paid chief reported to a board of fire commissioners, which approved requests for equipment and supplies needed to fight fires. Volunteer companies were given consecutive numbers as they formed, and those numbers are illustrated here.

VIGILANCE HOOK AND LADDER TRUCK AND CREW OUTSIDE OF THEIR STATION, C. 1877. Located at 720 Southwest Fourth Avenue, Vigilance was organized July 1853, making it the first viable volunteer company to serve in the Portland Fire Department.

10

THE CREW AND EQUIPMENT OF WILLAMETTE ENGINE NO. 1 OUTSIDE OF THEIR STATION, C. 1875. Located on Southwest Morrison Street between First and Second Avenues, Willamette was actually the second volunteer engine company (organized August 1853) to form but gained their No. 1 designation because Pioneer No. 1 did not become a working company after its initial formation in 1851.

A VOLUNTEER FROM WILLAMETTE NO. 1'S HOSE COMPANY POSING FOR A PORTRAIT, C. 1873. This image was taken by the company of Buchtel and Stolte. Joseph Buchtel was not only a photographer, but he was also fire chief for the volunteer force and PPFD. (Gohlston Collection.)

11

COLUMBIAN ENGINE NO. 3, C. 1880.
Located on Southwest Washington Street between Second and Third Avenues, Columbian was organized in June 1859. This image clearly illustrates handholds on the hose cart and hand-pump engine. Most engines were pulled by the volunteers themselves, as horses were a luxury that the city did not furnish in the early years. The city generally paid for hose and apparatus, but any extras were paid for by the companies themselves.

THOMAS JORDAN OF COLUMBIAN ENGINE NO. 3, 1875. Jordan was one of many early fire chiefs who rose from the ranks of volunteers to lead the fire department. He became the first chief of the PPFD.

FRONT COVER OF THE CONSTITUTION AND BY-LAWS FOR PROTECTION ENGINE NO. 4, 1873. Protection was the fourth viable engine company, with a formation date of October 1862.

CONSTITUTION

AND

By-Laws

OF

PROTECTION

ENGINE COMPANY No. 4.

Organized October 17, 1862; Admitted November 12, 1862;
Housed Steam Engine December 25, 1867.
New House erected in 1870. Destroyed by fire August 2d, 1873.

PORTLAND, OREGON:
A. G. WALLING, BOOK AND JOB PRINTER.
1873.

THE CREW, STATION, AND APPARATUS OF PROTECTION ENGINE NO. 4, C. 1880. Organized in October 1862, Protection was located at 1233 Southwest First Avenue. It appears that the engine at the time of this image was hand drawn, as there is no indication of horses or a harness system.

A STEAM ENGINE ON SOUTHWEST THIRD AVENUE, C. 1875. This volunteer engine crew has horses to pull their engine, a luxury in the early years. The engine is drafting from a cistern. The City of Portland spent much time and money creating an infrastructure of cisterns for firefighting before the wide use of fire hydrants made them obsolete.

FRONT COVER OF THE CONSTITUTION AND BY-LAWS FOR EAST PORTLAND'S GRANT ENGINE COMPANY, 1885. East Portland never had a paid fire department of its own, but with the consolidation of Portland, East Portland, and Albina in 1891, many East Portland volunteers worked their way onto the PPFD rolls.

A COMPOSITE OF THE MEMBERS AND THEIR STEAM ENGINE FROM EAST PORTLAND'S PIONEER ENGINE, C. 1880. At least one of these volunteers, T. DeBoest, became a member of the PPFD and in fact went on to become chief. This later image of the collage was taken in 1892, shortly after East Portland's consolidation with Portland.

ALBINA VOLUNTEER FIRE COMPANY NO. 1, 1890. Upon the consolidation of 1891, Portland's fire-protection area more than doubled in size, and volunteer companies like this one provided experienced firefighters who helped expand the paid ranks.

ALBINA VOLUNTEER FIRE COMPANY No. 1.   ORGANIZED 1883.   RE-ORGANIZED JULY 28, 1886.

15

VOLUNTEER HOSE COMPANY LOCATED ON NORTH MISSISSIPPI AVENUE, 1895. Even though the PPFD formed in 1883, volunteer companies continued to thrive in many parts of the city. This company continued the tradition of volunteerism in what was the former city of Albina.

HOSE-AND-CHEMICAL NO. 2 OF THE PPFD, 1896. Located on Southwest First Avenue, this paid company occupied the house of the former volunteer Protection No. 4. In this era of the PPFD, volunteers still helped supplement the ranks of companies such as this one. This image shows four paid crew members, including Capt. William R. Kerrigan (second from left). At the time, any of the nonuniformed individuals could have been volunteers at the station.

Front Cover of the Constitution and By-Laws for the Veteran Volunteer Firemen's Association, 1892. This organization was formed to assist volunteer firefighters with introductions to new stations and to assist former volunteers with personal needs, such as medical care. One of the founding members was Robert Holman, who was chief of the volunteer and paid departments.

CONSTITUTION
—and—
BY-LAWS
—of the—

VETERAN VOLUNTEER

FIREMEN'S ASSOCIATION

OF PORTLAND, OR.

ORGANIZED MAY 23D, 1889.

PORTLAND OREGON
CHAS F McDONALD COMMERCIAL JOB PRINTER
1892

Veteran Volunteer Firemen's Association Grand Ball Invitation, 1896. The major fundraiser for the Veteran Volunteers was an annual ball. In this instance, the invitation is illustrated with an image of two volunteers and a hand-pump engine.

VETERAN VOLUNTEER.....
FIREMENS ASSOCIATION
SIXTH AND
WASHINGTON STS.

GRAND BALL GIVEN AT

HIBERNIAN HALL
.....Tuesday Evening, May 19, 1896

SELLWOOD VOLUNTEER FIRE COMPANY NO. 1, LOCATED AT 8210 SOUTHEAST THIRTEENTH AVENUE, C. 1904. Many volunteer companies formed in areas that felt underserved by the PPFD. That seems to have been borne out in this case, as in 1907, the paid department installed Hose No. 4 in this same building.

THE TREMONT VOLUNTEER FIRE DEPARTMENT, 1913. Organized in December 1912, the station was located at Southeast Seventy-second Street and Knight Avenue. The crew includes, from left to right, the following: A. B. Strowbridge, president; Peter Wiser, chief; Frank Linderman, foreman; Victor Flink, assistant foreman; W. L. Goodman, pipeman; J. Zimmerman, pipeman; F. E. Foot, vice president; P. A. Kirchheimer, hydrant man; and L. Russell, press agent.

THE LENTS VOLUNTEER FIRE DEPARTMENT, LOCATED AT SOUTHEAST NINETY-THIRD AVENUE AND RAMONA STREET, 1914. Lents was an unincorporated area outside of Portland city limits at the time and was not near many Portland stations. This image illustrates that, even as the 20th century progressed, there was still a mix of motorized and hand-drawn apparatus in volunteer companies. (Nelson Photo Archive.)

THE ST. JOHNS VOLUNTEER FIRE DEPARTMENT, C. 1914. St. Johns was annexed to Portland in 1915. The station was located in the basement of St. Johns City Hall, and the volunteer department was replaced with Engine No. 32, which operated out of the same quarters.

WOODSTOCK VOLUNTEER HOSE COMPANY, C. 1916. This company was located on Southeast Sixtieth Avenue north of Woodstock Boulevard. After the Portland Fire Department went fully paid in 1904, it continued to supply such companies with hose but otherwise offered little assistance. (Gohlston Collection.)

WORLD WAR II AUXILIARY FIREFIGHTERS CONDUCTING PRACTICE DRILLS, C. 1943. World War II brought about a resurgence in volunteer firefighting. With the depletion of front-line firefighters and a fear that enemy bombing would overwhelm the peacetime infrastructure, volunteers were added to bolster the ranks. In September 1941, there were 1,156 people training to be auxiliary firefighters. These auxiliary units were designated with reserve numbers and were not integrated with front-line units.

ERROLL HEIGHTS VOLUNTEER FIREFIGHTERS, 1949. The Erroll Heights Station was located at Southeast Fifty-second Avenue and Ogden Street. At this time, Erroll Heights was near the border of Clackamas County and the City of Portland, making it an area that was not very close to the nearest paid fire station.

CIVIL DEFENSE AUXILIARY FIREFIGHTERS AND CHIEFS AT STATION NO. 20, 1953. This company was based at Station No. 20, a two-bay house that did not have a truck and thus had room for Civil Defense apparatus. On the right is Division Chief Walter Phillips, whose nephew William Phillips was a front-line firefighter at the time.

21

CIVIL DEFENSE AUXILIARY FIREFIGHTERS' PICNIC, 1954. Auxiliary area chief Alfred Kaiser presents an award to a firefighter at the annual auxiliary picnic at Columbia Park. As the World War II auxiliaries, Civil Defense–era volunteer firefighters were a separate branch of the fire department and often had little interaction with front-line personnel.

CIVIL DEFENSE AUXILIARY FIRE APPARATUS AT COLUMBIA PARK, C. 1957. Also on hand is the Stevens Car (white apparatus), which was equipped with loudspeakers that were used for announcements and also to broadcast music at various events. Notice the Civil Defense decals on the windshield of the front apparatus.

Two

THE EARLY ERA
(1883–1920)

The volunteer Portland Fire Department became the Portland Paid Fire Department (PPFD) in 1883. This change resulted from the rapid growth of the city and the fire of August 2, 1873, dubbed "Black Saturday." Considered Portland's greatest conflagration, it burned 22 city blocks to ashes. Another major transition was the 1891 consolidation of the cities of Portland, East Portland, and Albina, which forced a rapid expansion of the PPFD.

Five chiefs would serve the PPFD during its first 12 years, but it wasn't until 1895 that the most notable change in leadership would occur. David Campbell had spent much of his childhood chasing fire engines. He became a volunteer and, after the formation of the PPFD in 1883, worked his way up to first assistant to Chief Joseph Buchtel. On June 1, 1895, he was selected to replace the aging Buchtel. This was truly the changing of an era, as David Campbell would progressively lead the department over the next 16 years and secure his place in the history of Portland Fire & Rescue.

This early era was a very political time. City leaders and the board of commissioners often clashed over how the fire department should operate. With no civil-service rules as we know them today, appointments and firings were common. Chief Campbell was not immune to this and was removed from his position as chief in 1896 only to be reappointed in 1898 under a new administration.

In 1903, a civil-service system was implemented. This brought about the formation of the fully paid fire department in 1904. Funding for the first modern fireboat, the *George H. Williams*, was also secured. Launched in early 1904, it introduced an entirely new dimension to the fire department.

Another monumental change was the shift from horse-drawn fire apparatus to motorized vehicles. David Campbell recognized the advantages of speed and efficiency and purchased the first vehicle, his own chief's car, in 1909. The performance was so good that by 1911, the last horse-drawn vehicle was purchased. The transition progressed rapidly, and by April 1920, the department was fully motorized.

MEMBERS OF THE PORTLAND FIRE DEPARTMENT PULLING A HOSE CART ON SOUTHWEST THIRD AVENUE, 1888. This image was taken during the timed race at the annual "firemen's tournament" featuring local fire departments. This was the last time the event was held in Portland and also featured teams from East Portland, Vancouver, Albany, Lebanon, and Corvallis. Although the Portland department had done away with hand-drawn apparatus, teams were formed to partake in such competitions. This team included future chief David Campbell and longtime assistant chief Mike Laudenklos.

A PORTLAND PAID FIRE DEPARTMENT (PPFD) DRIVER, C. 1887. This image is unique because it shows the "PPFD Driver" insignia as a patch, not a badge. Images of this vintage usually show firefighters wearing metal badges bearing numbers. The patch, combined with his striped tie, illustrates the more flexible regulations during the early era.

FIRE APPARATUS TAKE PART IN A PARADE, 1891. This parade was staged during the visit of Pres. Benjamin Harrison. This view is at the intersection of Southwest First Avenue and Taylor Street.

HOSE COMPANY NO. 3 AT THEIR STATION, LOCATED AT 1917 SOUTHEAST SEVENTH AVENUE, C. 1894. The man standing on the wagon (right) is Capt. Lee Holden, who went on to become chief of the department. Holden began his career in 1887 as a volunteer in the East Portland Fire Department. After the consolidation of 1891, Holden was made captain at the newly established PPFD Hose No. 3. The battalion chief standing in front of Holden is Tinnies DeBoest, who also began his career as an East Portland volunteer and served as chief of the PPFD for two years. At this time, the PPFD still had volunteers in its ranks as well as extramen. A foreman and one other full-time firefighter were assigned to most apparatus, with extramen filling out the rest of the ranks. An extraman was "part paid" and was allowed to do outside work, but when the alarm bell sounded, he was expected to make his way to the fire.

STATION NO. 9, 1897. This image documents the political nature of the late-19th-century fire department. Located at 720 Southwest Fourth Avenue, this station was originally built as Station No. 1 in 1890 and remained so until 1921 with one exception. After the department's administrative staff was let go upon the election of a new mayor in 1896, the new chief decided to renumber Station No. 1. This was done in 1897 and lasted less than a year, for when Chief Campbell was reinstated in 1898, he changed it back to Station No. 1. The change to Station No. 9 was in name only, as none of the crew or apparatus changed after it was done. If you look closely at the new numbers five and nine, you can see that they are brighter than the words "truck" and "engine." The engine is a second-class Clapp & Jones.

TRUCK NO. 1 OUTSIDE OF THE COUNTY COURTHOUSE AT SOUTHWEST FOURTH AVENUE AND SALMON STREET, 1899. As an illustration of a fire horse's durability, this team was still together in 1905, and the two darker horses were still pulling Truck No. 1 at the time they were replaced by a tractor-driven ladder in 1913. The truck is a first-class Hayes.

FIREFIGHTERS AND OFFICERS INSIDE STATION NO. 7, LOCATED AT 302 SOUTHEAST THIRD AVENUE, 1900. Seated from left to right are William Morrison, Dan Penney, George Stewart, and Lee Holden. Standing are Andy Powell, Fred Robinson, Warren Smith, Dan McGrew, and Fred W. Roberts. Battalion Chief Holden became chief of the department, and Extraman Roberts became fire marshal. George Stewart is wearing a rarely seen badgeless hat that reads "PPFD Engineer."

TRUCK NO. 4, 1900. At the time of this image, Truck No. 4 was located at 420 Northeast Holladay Street and had its own station. During the early era, there were many single-apparatus stations, as traditions from the volunteer era were slow to change. As the early era progressed, stations were erected with double- and triple-apparatus bays, and trucks were paired with engines. However, it was not until 1984 that trucks and engines would share the same station number. The driver is William Heath, who later became a battalion chief; the first person to his right is Extraman Isaac N. Williams. The truck is a third-class Hayes.

HOSE NO. 2, 1900. As was the case in the early years, the driver and the foreman in this image are the only full-time firefighters on the crew. The four extramen were on call and could work outside the station. However, the extramen had the option of living at the station, as did all four pictured here. Seated from left to right are driver John H. Price, David Kerrigan, and Foreman William Kerrigan. A foreman was equivalent to the rank of captain. In the early 20th century, a full-time firefighter seldom left the station for long periods of time.

TRAINING EXERCISE WITH POMPIER LADDERS, 1903. Prior to having dedicated training facilities, the fire department used available tall buildings for drilling. Here Chief David Campbell (left) looks on while firefighters take a break from drilling on the back side of the old Exposition Building. The Exposition Building backed up to Multnomah Field, where various sports events were held. In the lower right corner are the words "M. A. A. C. opponent," signifying that the lower level of the building was used as the Multnomah Amateur Athletic Club's opponent's locker room. Notice the life net behind the training dummy. Later firefighters have complained that life nets were rarely used other than in training and that being on the receiving end of a jumper was not pleasant, as it was rough on arms, shoulders, and backs. However, in earlier times, they were used, and Portland has one of the highest life-net rescues on record. During the Chamber of Commerce Building fire in 1906, a person jumped seven stories into a net, breaking the net and two of his ribs but otherwise living to tell the tale.

HARNESSING HORSES TO A HOSE CART, C. 1910. In the early era, horses and men worked as teams to ensure a quick response to fires. Once harnessed, the only thing that slowed horse-drawn apparatus was distance. On longer runs, the horses had to be walked a short distance in order to regain their wind. Once at the fire, horses were unhitched and had to be walked in order to cool down. This task was often done by bystanders while the firefighters were busy. During the early years, stations were sited with consideration given to how far and fast horses could run as well as how hilly or flat the service area was. As motorized apparatus became more prevalent, these considerations became a thing of the past. During the early 20th century, all new horses were broken in at department headquarters, located at Southwest Fourth Avenue and Taylor Street. Chief Edward Grenfell later stated: "Frazier and McLean had a livery stable at Fifth and Taylor and supplied most of the horses. Most of them were unbroken horses from Eastern Oregon." The firefighter with the reins in his hands is Herman A. Bates.

INTERIOR VIEW OF APPARATUS HARNESS AND CREW AT STATION NO. 11, C. 1907. When the bell sounded, the horses would walk into position, the driver would pull the rope above his seat, and the harnesses would drop onto the horses' backs. Another firefighter would go to the head of the horse and snap the collar shut, and the team was ready in a matter of seconds. The firefighter on the right is Herman A. Bates.

A HOSE WAGON IN ACTION, C. 1909. Once the horses were harnessed, they eagerly powered the apparatus to the fire. The journey was not a quiet one, as a bell combined with the noise of the galloping horses and steel tires on the road made a great amount of noise.

ENGINE AND HOSE NO. 6 IN NORTHWEST PORTLAND, C. 1903. The department often attempted to match a station's horses by size and color and, in this instance, met with success. The engine is a fourth-class Silsby. (Nelson Photo Archive.)

THE LEWIS AND CLARK EXPOSITION FIRE DEPARTMENT, 1905. The exposition grounds were so large and far away from the downtown stations that a station was set up to serve on site and was comprised of members of the Portland Fire Department on special detail. The station was located just inside the front entrance, and the department responded to 30 alarms from February to November. Chief of the Exposition Department Benjamin F. Dowell is the passenger on the ladder truck.

ENGINE NO. 4 AT A FIRE, 1909. Capt. J. B. Simpson oversees operations as Engineer Charles Winters runs their first-class Metropolitan engine. At this time, Engine No. 4 was located at 1724 Southwest Fourth Avenue. As an illustration of how all-encompassing being a firefighter was during the single-platoon era, all of the crew during 1909 had residences on either Southwest Fourth or Fifth Avenues. The majority lived within one or two blocks, and four listed the station as their residence. Part of being a firefighter in the early era meant that one lived in or near the station to which he was assigned; as a result, many a firefighter served his entire career at one station.

FIRE ON SOUTHEAST GRAND AVENUE AND YAMHILL STREET, 1909. This working fire scene at the U.S. Laundry Company shows firefighters in action, including a three-man ladder carry and a charged-up steam engine. Note the firefighter on the back left side of the ladder has his helmet turned backward. Prior to the use of modern face shields, firefighters often turned their helmets in such a fashion to guard against the fire's heat and for greater protection from falling debris.

ENGINE NO. 3 FIGHTING A FIRE AT SOUTHWEST TWELFTH AVENUE AND WASHINGTON STREET, 1910. Fires and firefighters in action have always drawn crowds of onlookers, as demonstrated in this early fire scene. Chief Edward Grenfell later noted, "In the early days we had no fire prevention laws. It was all done through cooperation, and that cooperation was not very good."

TRUCK NO. 3 TURNING FROM NORTHWEST FOURTEENTH AVENUE ONTO GLISAN STREET, 1911. The truck is a first-size American LaFrance combination.

NEW HOSE-AND-CHEMICAL ENGINE 22, JUNE 6, 1913. Taken a month after the new motorized engine's purchase, this image also shows the "horse power" that the new engine was to replace looking on from the stalls at the back of the apparatus floor. The engine is an American LaFrance Type 10 combination hose-and-chemical.

Horse-Drawn Truck No. 1 with Crew outside of Station No. 1, July 14, 1913. The apparatus is a third-class Hayes. The increase in the paving of roads during the early 20th century contributed to the rapid demise of horse-drawn apparatus. Horses and pavement did not always make a good mix, as falls were more common than on dirt. In 1910, Chief Campbell stated, "For the paved street districts, especially on long runs, the auto service is far superior." During the horse era, this station is where horses were broken into firefighting work. Chief Edward Grenfell later described how this was done: "You'd take a new horse and put him in the center of a three-horse hitch with a good steady team. You'd put a man behind him with a long whip and when the bell rang he'd give him a few sharp cracks. Pretty soon when the bell rang that horse would get out fast. First he'd think he was running away. We'd go up 4th Avenue and turn up Jefferson and hit that Jefferson hill. With a good heavy rig on, by the time we got up to Broadway and Jefferson he'd be jumping straight up and down. It didn't take long to break 'em in."

MOTORIZED TRACTOR-DRIVEN TRUCK NO. 1 AND CREW OUTSIDE OF STATION NO. 1, JULY 14, 1913. This image was taken along with the previous one from this date to document "the old and the new." It nicely illustrates the transition from horse-drawn to motorized apparatus, as the crew is the same in each image. The truck is an 85-foot aerial truck pulled by a Type 16 American LaFrance tractor. As hydraulic ladders came later in the 20th century, firefighters who had used these spring-mechanism ladders stated that they were often faster than the modern versions, as the spring load would propel the ladder up about halfway very quickly with no effort. Firefighters would then use this momentum to crank it up the rest of the way. The man standing on the truck is Battalion Chief Lee Holden, who later became chief of the department. The man second from the left on the ground is Howard Gill, who became a battalion chief and chief training officer.

DRIVER GEORGE HOLSHEIMER AND CREW POSE ON THE APRON AT STATION NO. 9, 1914.
Located at Southeast Thirty-fifth Avenue and Belmont Street, Engine No. 9 was a 1911 American LaFrance. This engine was the first motorized firefighting apparatus purchased by the city. In 1913, Capt. William Kerrigan of Station No. 15 stated, "I entered the Portland fire service when they used hand machines, served until they got horses, and now am serving on automobile apparatus. When they get flying machines I am going to quit."

THE FIRE DEPARTMENT'S MACHINE SHOP, 1915. In addition to maintaining and assembling apparatus and equipment, the department's mechanics and carpenters fabricated many items used by firefighters. These included items as varied as ladders, station furniture, and windshields for apparatus.

40

COVER OF THE FIRE DEPARTMENT BAND'S NATIONAL TOUR SCHEDULE, 1913. The band was a fixture of the department in the early 20th century and during this nationwide tour stopped at the White House to meet and pose for pictures with President Wilson. Later trumpeter and band director Capt. Alex Holden and other band members formed a private band called Captain Holden and His Smoke Eaters.

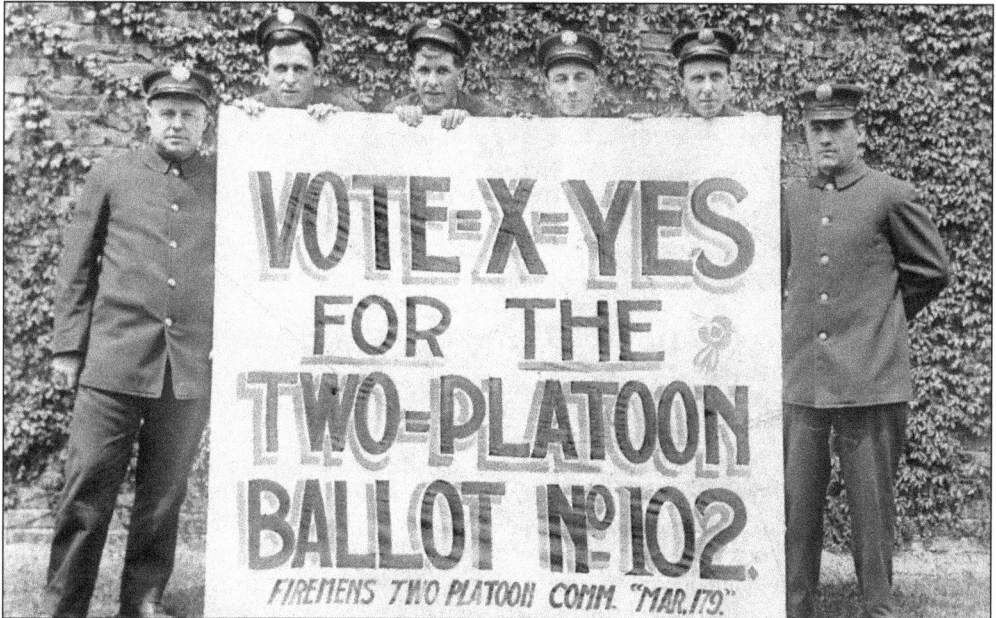

FIREFIGHTERS CAMPAIGN FOR THE TWO-PLATOON SYSTEM, MAY 1917. Although they did not win their campaign in that year's special election, they went on to succeed the following year.

Reliable Information

ABOUT

Two-Platoon in Portland, Ore.

FACTS

Number of additional men required to install two-platoon......92
    (An increase of 22½ per cent.)

Amount of money required less than.....................$90,000
    (An increase of about 17½ per cent.)

UNTRUTHS

By Press and Fire Bureau Officials

Double the number of men will be required for two-platoon.
    (There are now 419 in the department.)
That $200,000 to $300,000 additional will be required.

SOMEBODY IS WRONG

Don't Take Anybody's Word

Investigate For Yourself

The two-platoon is endorsed by the most progressive Chiefs in our country and is opposed, as a rule, only by those who are not broad enough to get out of the old rut.

Of twenty-one (21) cities having a per capita loss during 1915, of less than one dollar ($1.00), **seven** (7) of them are two-platoon cities, and of the twenty-nine (29) cities having a per capita loss of more than five (5) dollars, **not one** belongs in the two-platoon column.

How Is This For Fire Protection?

Seven Two-Platoon Cities out of a possible 32 stand in the highest class against thousands under the old system.

Two-Platoon Campaign Committee

JAS. IRVING   Jolly-Ratelle, Printers 269 Washington St.   312 Gerlinger
Sec'y.   Bldg.

A FLYER FROM THE TWO-PLATOON CAMPAIGN COMMITTEE, 1918. The creation of the two-platoon system was one of the major changes during the early era of the fire department. It was also a very contentious issue and was seen by many as a labor/management struggle, with many chiefs either not supportive or overtly against the idea. This led to many confrontations in the local media and to a campaign by the firefighters to garner support through various avenues, including flyers such as this one. The implementation of a two-platoon system required a charter amendment that was defeated by voters in June 1917 and May 1918 before finally passing in November 1918.

Three

THE MODERN ERA
(1921–1980)

The Fire Prevention Bureau was established in 1918, with Jay Stevens becoming its first fire marshal. In 1922, they embarked on a major initiative to remove dilapidated buildings from the city. This, along with other fire-prevention initiatives and a workforce of fire inspectors, reduced fire loss to the city and proved a valuable addition to the department.

This era saw continued efforts to standardize training and increase professionalism in Portland's fire-and-rescue services. Rescue services began with the creation of Squad No. 1 (first aid and rescue) in the early 1920s; the Portland Fire College was established in 1930; a drill tower was completed in 1936; and the first company dedicated to training new recruits was created in 1953.

Work shifts continued to change during this era. Prior to 1910, firefighters worked seven-day weeks with 12 hours off per week. In 1910, their time off doubled to 24 hours per week. In 1918, a two-platoon system was implemented, and firefighters began working 24 hours on duty and 24 hours off in a continual rotation. In 1948, a third platoon was added, which reduced the 72-hour workweek to 56 hours.

The war years between 1940 and 1945 brought new challenges for the department. During this period, 50 percent of the trained firefighting force entered military service. Chief Edward Grenfell noted that 10 people lost their lives to fire during fiscal year 1943–1944, a 300-percent increase over the peacetime average, and the amount of property lost to fire amounted to more than the total fire loss for the six years prior to the war.

Between 1957 and 1963, a modernization program reconfigured fire department operations. The number of stations was reduced from 38 to 30, and many new apparatus were purchased to update an aging fleet.

Other forms of technology would change the face of the fire department as well. Lightweight hose and hose couplings would make their entrance in 1966. Two years later, full-protection helmets would also be added. By 1972, self-contained breathing apparatus would replace filter masks in one of the most significant changes the fire service would recognize.

PORTLAND FIRE COLLEGE, 1930. Battalion Chief Edward Boatright established the Fire College in 1930 to bring more standardized training to the department. The college operated until 1943 and produced the department's first training manuals—the original was dubbed the "Boatright Bible." Standing from left to right are Battalion Chiefs Henry Johnson and Benton French; Fire Marshal Fred Roberts; Chief Edward Grenfell; Battalion Chief William Heath; two unidentified men; Capt. Willis Smith; and Boatright.

MOVIE STAR MARY PICKFORD POSES FOR THE DEPARTMENT'S MILK FUND CAMPAIGN, 1935. In 1932, Lt. (also known as Junior Captain at that time) Fred Roberts began a campaign to provide pasteurized milk to young children in order to prevent illness. Many well-known celebrities helped Roberts get the message out. To Pickford's right are Mayor Joseph Carson and Fire Marshal Fred Roberts, and on the ground to her left is Fire Commissioner Earl Riley.

THE NEW FIRE ALARM TELEGRAPH BUILDING, 1931. In 1930, the Fire Alarm Telegraph Office moved into its own building, located at Northeast Twenty-first Avenue and Pacific Street, after spending the prior 32 years in the basement of city hall.

FIRE ALARM TELEGRAPH LINE CREW AT WORK, C. 1952. In this image, the lineman is assisted by Harry Heise (right) and the crew of Engine No. 12. The line crews were responsible for maintaining a large network of fire-alarm boxes. With telephones becoming ubiquitous in homes and businesses, fire-alarm boxes became obsolete. In 1977, the department decommissioned the 651 boxes that remained in residential areas.

FIRE DEPARTMENT BASEBALL TEAM, C. 1938. The department fielded many athletes and teams that competed at local and regional levels. They played for charitable purposes, fitness, and healthy competition. Pictured from left to right are (first row) ? Endicott, Vernon Rayley, George Wallace, Robert Cunningham, and ? Scrivner; (second row) Arnold Gabriel, Terry Schrunk, Francis Desbouillons, Thomas Mayer, LaVelle Desbouillons, unidentified, John Wanner, and Ernest Shipley.

ACCIDENT AT SOUTHWEST FOURTH AVENUE AND OAK STREET, 1943. While responding to a fire, Compressor and Engine No. 1 collided in downtown Portland. Responding to emergencies can prove hazardous to firefighters, and in this case, nine were injured. The introduction of faster motorized apparatus in the early 20th century made collisions such as this one—and others with private vehicles—more common than they are today. Such incidents lessened as better communications and signaling, along with heightened public awareness of emergency procedures, grew.

46

MELVIN WILKENING AT A FIRE, 1946.
Wilkening takes a moment to pose with
a new self-contained breathing apparatus
(SCBA) at Southwest First Avenue
and Taylor Street. As the modern era
progressed, the department began to
use filter masks similar to those used
by the military for gas attacks and then
began using SCBAs. As late as 1939, the
department had only one filter mask per
apparatus, but even then firefighters were
not required to use them.

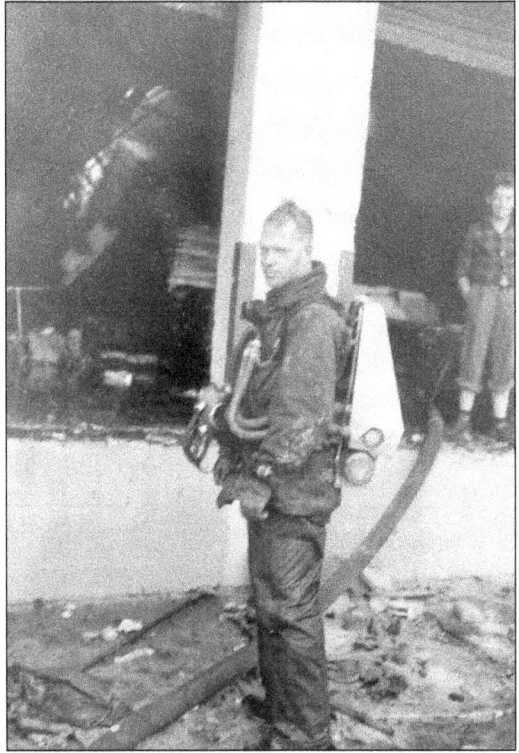

**WALTER KURATH (LEFT) AND GALE
BUCHANAN PREPARE TO WORK THE
FISHER BODY FIRE, 1948.** The name
"smoke eater" was well earned in the early
days of firefighting. Before the wide use
of SCBAs, filter masks were a firefighter's
only defense against such smoke. However,
the masks still did not make up for the lack
of oxygen in smoke, and a firefighter was
susceptible to the effects of too little of it.

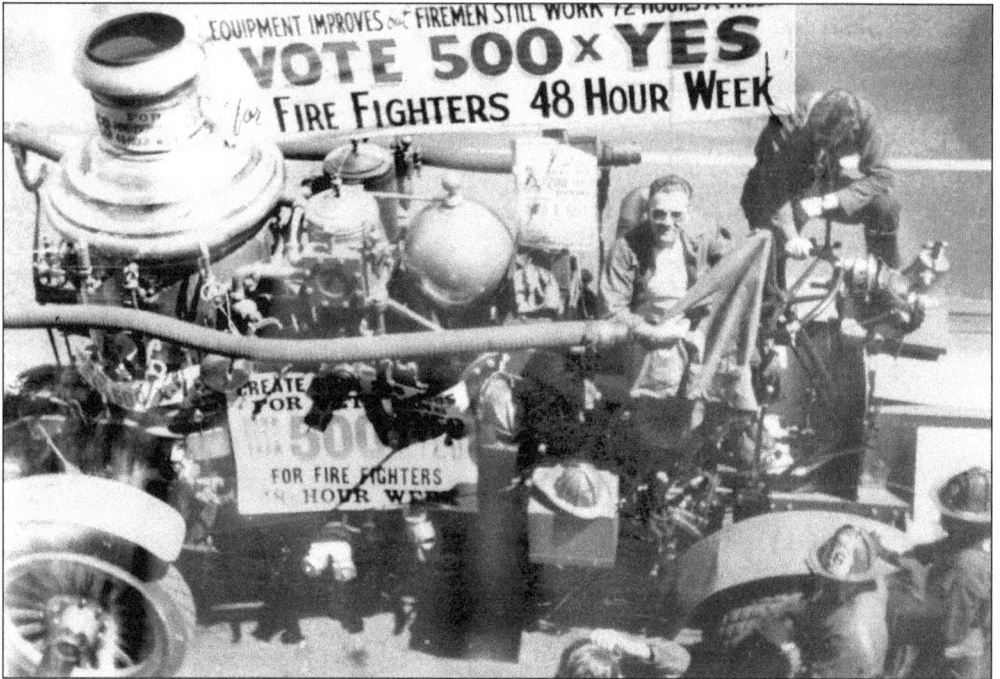

CAMPAIGNING FOR 48-HOUR WEEK, 1946. Orville Baker takes a ride on a steam engine to campaign for the three-platoon system. This campaign for a 48-hour work week did not succeed in the May election, but in November, the voters passed a similar measure that brought about a 60-hour workweek, creating a need for the three-platoon system that exists today. Future chief Dale Gilman was elected to head the campaign.

TRUCK NO. 7 ON NORTH INTERSTATE AVENUE JUST NORTH OF STATION NO. 24, 1948. This campaign for new equipment was held during Fire Prevention Week, and many of the department's older vehicles were draped with similar banners. The "City Service Truck" is a 1922 Seagrave. The driver is Cecil Norris, and seated next to him is Capt. Roy Geer.

NEW FAGEOL AND KENWORTH ENGINES DEMONSTRATING AT THE DEPARTMENT DRILL TOWER, 1939. The drill tower was completed in 1936 by the Works Progress Administration and was an instrumental part of the heightened effort to standardize training. Chief Dowell first proposed a drill tower in 1914, but the idea did not come to fruition until the 1930s. In this instance, the department shows off its 1938 engines, which were assembled in the local shop of Wentworth and Irwin and the department shops located at the drill-tower complex. The chassis were built to city specifications, and the bodies were assembled from standard parts. Fire Commissioner Riley claimed that the city saved $21,000 by assembling the engines locally rather than purchasing completed apparatus directly from the manufacturer.

THE FIRE DEPARTMENT DRILL TEAM AT THE DRILL TOWER, 1938. The drill team was active from 1937 to 1941 and trained and performed at the new drill tower. The team also performed during Pacific Coast Fire Chiefs' conventions in many Oregon and West Coast cities as well as in Salt Lake City. Full performances consisted of a one-and-a-half-hour show, including comedy, pompiering, and precision along with stunt life-line exhibitions. Separate educational demonstrations included hose-and-ladder evolutions and rescue procedures. Pictured from left to right are Ralph Miller, Lawrence Barzee, James Scott, Leo Weidner, Chester Klock, William McKinney, Tom Turlay, Clayton Thompson, James Riopelle, Vernon Rayley, and Samuel Steele.

AN ENGINE NO. 2 TRAINING COMPANY AT CENTRAL STATION DRILL TOWER, 1959. Established in 1953, the Engine No. 2 training company was the first attempt to standardize training for all new appointees to the department. Prior to this, recruits served a one-year probation at the station to which they were appointed. It was up to the captain of that station to train the rookie firefighter and, as a result, training varied widely. Under the new program, the trainees served on the training engine for six months. Pictured from left to right are driver Everett Marl, officer Cecil Norris, Harold Richards, Maurice Thompson, Ben Sickinger, Larry Miles, and Merrill Gonterman. Training and practice evolved as the 20th century progressed. In 1955, Chief Edward Grenfell described some of the differences: "In the old days we just poured the water on, knocked the fire down and went home. We didn't think about salvage. There has been a great saving in property in the salvage work we've done in the last 20 to 25 years."

TRAINING AT THE CENTRAL STATION DRILL TOWER, 1956. Central Station's drill tower was not used as heavily as the original tower on Southeast Powell Boulevard. However, it was a convenient location for the training crews based at Engine No. 2. This is a group of "re-treads," front-line firefighters who had been appointed before the training company was established and were subsequently sent through training when there were not enough new appointees to fill the ranks. Here they have set up a safety net for repelling and are using pompier ladders. The loops on the firefighters' belts are for repelling. Not pictured here are the hose, axe, and life belts that were part of a firefighter's standard equipment. Portland's own Capt. Alvin Sherk patented and sold hose, axe, and life belts that were used nationwide. Pictured from left to right are Kenneth Carter, Charles Smith, Donald Hlebechuk, Bernard Ryan, Clark Stephens (on net), Donald Olander, and Training Officer Benjamin Steele (on ground).

Training at the Flammable Liquids Training Ground in Linnton, c. 1957. The grounds were built by oil and commercial companies and donated to the city. Many generations of Portland firefighters remember training at this site. According to Capt. Gale Buchanan, the department had an agreement with local petroleum companies to use rejected aviation fuel to supply the liquids for such practice sessions.

Charles Weberg Instructs Trainees at Station No. 23, c. 1970. Engine No. 23 replaced Engine No. 2 as the department's training company in 1960 and moved to a new station at the drill tower in 1961. New appointees faced a year of probationary training— six months each on Engine No. 23 and Truck No. 4—and then often spent time as "travelers" while waiting for a full-time appointment to a station.

A-Shift Training Crew at Station No. 23, 1976. At the time of this image, training crews consisted of eight appointees—four on the engine and four on the truck—the training officer, and apparatus operators. If a trainee was fired or quit during the probationary period, a front-line firefighter would take that person's place during drills requiring four people, as new appointees could not be added once the training cycle began. Pictured from left to right are (standing) driver Donald Hlebechuk; Tillerman Glen Eisner; trainees Edwin Morterud, Walter Turner, Edward Grenfell, William Shannon, and Roderick Fox; driver Arthur Schmidt; and officer August Stone; (kneeling) trainees Frank Mass, Rex Johanson, and Scott Gotter. In the early to mid-1970s, in addition to training at Station No. 23, the department accepted funds from the Federal Emergency Employment Act to help train "unemployed veterans and disadvantaged citizens." Old Station No. 24 on North Interstate Avenue was used as the home location for this program, which was named "Training 2." This program was designed to prepare trainees for department-entrance tests, and those who passed were then accepted into training at Station No. 23.

Four

UNIQUE FIRE AND
RESCUE APPARATUS

Fire apparatus remain one of the most recognizable features of Portland Fire & Rescue. Much time and effort is spent on the care and maintenance of these vehicles. In most cases, fire apparatus serve for about 25 years. Some exceptions have shown great longevity. One thing is certain—new or old, a shiny piece of fire equipment always draws public interest.

Over 150 years ago, they began as hand-drawn vehicles. They evolved to horse-drawn and, finally, to motorized vehicles. Today highly specialized fire-and-rescue vehicles can be found serving Portland.

The volunteer days began modestly. Horses were a very limited part of the picture, as they proved to be one of the most expensive elements for protecting the city. It wasn't until 1883 that the city's budget allowed for horses at every fire company.

The horse-drawn era was truly one of the most colorful and romantic periods for the fire service. A great fire horse was intelligent, courageous, and dedicated to service. While efforts were made to aesthetically match teams by size and color of horse, the great horses were most known for their abilities and performance.

The transition from horse to motorized apparatus spawned some unusual vehicles. "Hybrids" were developed as apparatus manufacturers, determined to maintain customer loyalty, would sell motorized tractors that could be attached to the horse-drawn vehicles after the front axles were removed. Eventually this gave way to purpose-built fire vehicles to meet the growing need for specialized equipment.

Numerous specialty vehicles have served Portland over the years, including rescue units, support vehicles, and fireboats (see Chapter Five). Some have had long and successful careers, while others were noted for immediate failure. Some have survived the decades and remain today as a testimony to past service.

Noted here are vehicles that were unique to Portland, firsts of their kind, and rarities in the department. Also noted are those vehicles, and adaptations to them, that were completed in the department's shops.

CHIEF DAVID CAMPBELL AND HIS DRIVER IN THE CHIEF'S CAR, C. 1910. This 1909 Pierce-Arrow was the first motorized vehicle purchased by the department and did much to convince Campbell that automobiles were more effective than horse-drawn apparatus. In one instance, Campbell loaded this car with firefighters and hose to respond to a fire in the west hills. He stated, "in a few minutes the automobile crew had reached the burning residence, hitched on to the neighboring hydrant with hose and nozzle, and put out the fire. This would have been impossible except for the chief's automobile."

RESERVE ENGINE NO. 2, 1937. This "hybrid" vehicle nicely demonstrates the transition from horse and steam to motorized apparatus. First the horses were replaced with a tractor, and as pumping engines became the norm, the steam engines were also phased out. This 1899 Metropolitan was the last steamer to serve in a front-line station in Portland.

ENGINE NO. 21 RESPONDS TO A FIRE, C. 1916. While not unique itself, this 1913 Pope Hartford Type M27 hose-and-chemical engine was one of only two Portland would purchase. Capt. William Heath (passenger seat) and his crew are seen here in Southwest Portland. Note the primitive fire-signal system on the pole at this intersection.

SQUAD NO. 1 DECORATED FOR THE ROSE FESTIVAL PARADE, C. 1926. This was the department's first "rescue" vehicle and marks the beginning of a long line of dedicated emergency-response vehicles in Portland. In 1924, it was converted in the department shops from a 1913 American LaFrance hose-and-chemical engine. Firefighter Joseph Penner is third from right.

SQUAD NO. 1, 1931. A 1928 Studebaker, this was the first new emergency-services vehicle purposely built for such work. Chief Lee Holden was responsible for the design, and the department shops built the body on a Studebaker chassis. In addition to their standard uniform markings, firefighters who served on the squad had Red Cross insignias on their uniforms.

58

THE BAKER FIRST AID CAR COMMITTEE, C. 1932. George Baker was Portland's first four-term mayor, and to honor him as he neared the end of his career, a group was formed to purchase and name a rescue vehicle after him. The committee obviously had a sense of humor and included Police Chief Leon Jenkins and Assistant Fire Chief James Dillane (first row second and fourth from left, respectively).

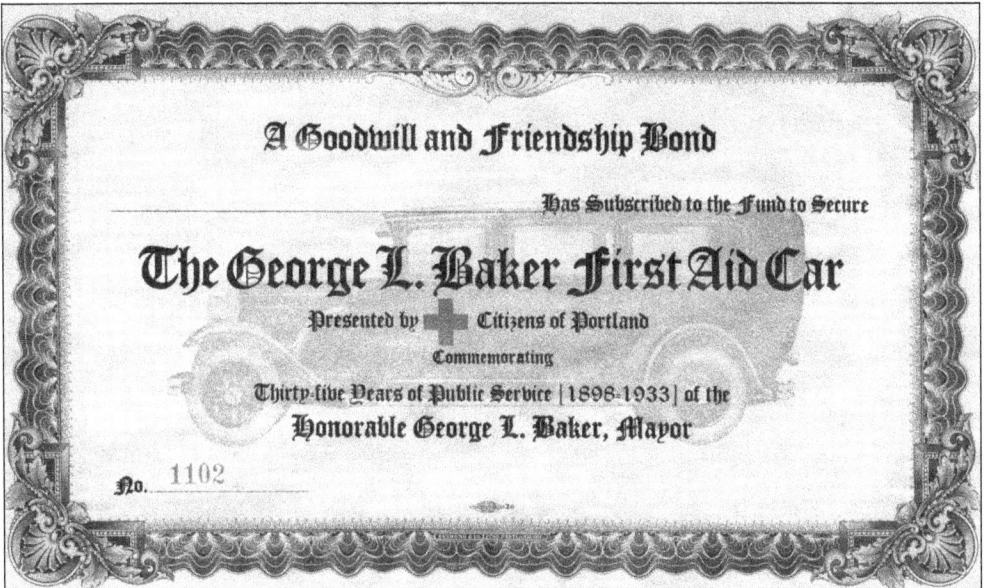

BAKER CAR BOND CERTIFICATE, 1932. The public was invited to contribute to the Baker Car campaign, and contributions could be made using these goodwill and friendship bonds.

THE FIRST BAKER CAR, 1932. The car was a 1932 Lincoln costing $2,470 and was placed at Station No. 1, located at 905 Southwest Fourth Avenue.

THE SECOND BAKER CAR, 1953. Paul Meyers (left) and Glen Whallon pose with the second Baker Car, a 1953 Chevrolet, outside of Central Station.

THE GRAND PREVIEW OF THE JAY W. STEVENS DISASTER UNIT INSIDE THE MUNICIPAL AUDITORIUM, 1939. No other piece of fire apparatus in Portland's history has seen such public attention and acclaim as the Stevens, and 5,000 people attended the ceremonies. Much of the unit's equipment was made to department specification in factories nationwide, and Capt. Alvin Sherk and firefighter Roy Love were given special detail in order to spec and purchase the equipment. Love went on to serve on the Stevens for all but five years of the unit's existence. The unit carried more than 1,200 pieces of equipment, including a two-way radio system, a lighting system, generators, and operating equipment. The unit was manned by firefighters who were qualified emergency medical technicians who had approximately 250 hours of classroom and practical emergency-care training. It was anticipated that the unit would be used on a regional basis, not just in Portland, and it was equipped to respond to rescues on Mount Hood, major accidents, landslides, floods, epidemics, explosions, mine and tunnel rescues, and even shipwrecks. It had a complete emergency hospital and room for transporting seven injured people.

INVITATION TO VIEW THE NEW STEVENS UNIT, 1939. Designated Rescue No. 1, the Stevens was purchased and equipped by local businessman Aaron Frank. The unit was built in the local shops of Wentworth and Irwin on a Kenworth chassis. It was named for Stevens, who had been fire marshal in Portland and went on to become a national leader in fire-prevention efforts during the first half of the 20th century.

THE STEVENS UNIT'S REDEDICATION AS THE JAY W. STEVENS EMERGENCY CAR, 1953. The Stevens had a long service life for the department, and Aaron Frank again donated money to upgrade the unit for the new civil-defense era. While not as big an event as the original rollout, the rededication outside of city hall was still well attended and widely covered by the local media.

THE STEVENS CAR AS COMMAND CENTER, 1968. The Stevens served as a command-and-control center on all greater alarm fires and was the place where off-shift firefighters checked in when responding to callbacks. The loudspeakers could be heard from two miles away, and the complete field kitchen and field hospital meant that firefighters had food and medical care without needing to leave the fire.

RESCUE NO. 1 UNDER CONSTRUCTION, 1971. The Stevens was in service until 1971, when it was replaced by this 1972 Dodge. This unit was outfitted and equipped by Lt. Frank Oliverio and was affectionately dubbed "Oli's Folly" and the "Motor Home." At the rear of the rescue are Assistant Chief Peter Leinweber (left) and firefighter James Havelhurst.

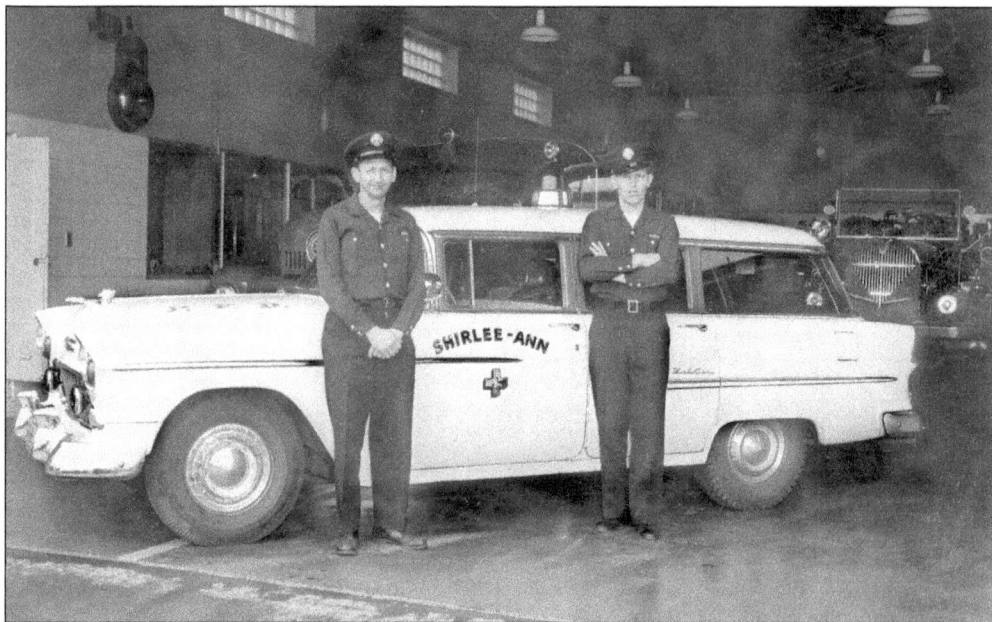

SHIRLEE ANN RESCUE CAR, 1960. Warren Messick (left) and Merrill Gonterman pose with the original Shirlee Ann, which was based at Station No. 22. Also known as Rescue No. 3, the car was purchased by the citizens of St. Johns after a young girl, Shirlee Ann Howell, died for the lack of emergency services in the area. The community raised money and created the Shirlee Ann Fund, purchasing this Chevrolet wagon in 1956.

REFURBISHMENT CEREMONY FOR THE SECOND SHIRLEE ANN, 1975. This version was a 1972 Dodge van. Pictured from left to right are Chief Gordon Morterud, Fire Commissioner Charles Jordan, James Wattenbarger, and Robert McEuin. Although a rescue unit is no longer located in St. Johns, the Shirlee Ann Fund still exists today and is used to purchase needed equipment for Station No. 22.

TRUCK NO. 8 OUTSIDE OF STATION NO. 16, C. 1940. Located at 1436 Southwest Montgomery Street, this unit was a Kenworth City Service Truck that was built by Wentworth and Irwin and the department shops. It carried the first aluminum ladders used in the department and was dubbed "too modern" by some older firefighters. A City Service Truck is a truck that has no aerial ladder but carries many other types of ladders.

THE "DOUBLE BUBBLE," C. 1952. Bruce Cullen (left) and Frank Getch sit behind Engine No. 12's "double bubble" windshield. In the early years, apparatus did not come equipped with windshields. The department's shops manufactured many of these double bubbles for apparatus of all kinds, taking vehicles from the earlier era and giving them a unique Portland Fire Department look.

ENGINE NO. 19, 1954. Engine No. 19 (right), a 1954 Seagrave quadruple engine, was the only one of its kind owned by Portland. Note the double bubble on the reserve engine, a 1918 American LaFrance.

CHEMICAL NO. 1, C. 1965. This 1938 Fageol was converted by the department shops into a chemical engine in 1965. The image was taken at the Flammable Liquids Training Ground in Linnton.

TANKER NO. 1, C. 1968. This tanker was placed at Station No. 6, located at 3660 Northwest Front Avenue. Tankers are a rarity in Portland because rural firefighting is not the norm. Station No. 6 is near Forest Park (located in Portland's northwest hills), which the department is responsible for protecting. This unit had a 1,350-gallon tank and also carried forest-firefighting tools.

DEDICATION CEREMONY FOR THE JEFF MORRIS FIRE SAFETY EDUCATION UNIT, 1975. After Morris's death, the Friends of Jeff Morris Committee was established to help continue his public-education efforts. Attending the ceremony are Morris's widow Lila (with dalmatian) and Chief Gordon Morterud (seated next to her).

THE MORRIS UNIT, 1975. Here the unit, a 1971 Ford, is parked at the Skidmore Fountain in Southwest Portland. The donation agreement stated that the van was to be used exclusively for fire-prevention education programs.

Five

FIREBOATS

Sitting at the confluence of two major waterways that connect Oregon to the Pacific Ocean, it was inevitable that Portland would become a major shipping port. Logged to make room for a growing city, old-growth timber became the primary building material in Portland. In the mid-1880s, fire from both man and nature was a constant threat. Recognizing this, Thomas Dryer organized the first group of volunteer firefighters in Portland.

The waterways, however, added another dimension. Because of the reliance on the rivers, particularly the Willamette as it flowed to the Columbia, Portland would find piers and wharfs critical to its economy. Keeping these facilities safe and operational was of utmost importance.

Chief David Campbell recognized and promoted the need for fireboats vigorously. Campbell's vision was realized on February 27, 1904, when the first modern fireboat, the *George H. Williams*, was christened for service. Named for the sitting mayor, the *Williams* would be the first of many fireboats to serve Portland.

Portland fireboats were originally intended only to fight fires. As building materials, fire codes, and experience improved, Portland's waterfronts became safer. By 1973, this reality brought the addition of harbor-patrol duties, formerly conducted by the police bureau, to the fireboat agenda. Reduced criminal activity on the waterways helped mold this decision, but it was not without its share of political controversy.

In more modern times, fireboat duties have been expanded to support dive-and-rescue services particular to rivers. Fireboats have become smaller, faster, and more maneuverable, but the special nature of their service to Portland remains unchanged after more than a century.

STEAM ENGINES ON BARGES, 1894. Although not officially fireboats, Chief Campbell had engines put on barges during the flood of 1894 in order to serve areas that were otherwise unreachable. Chief Campbell was a proponent of fireboats, but it would take him 10 more years to make his vision a reality.

PORTLAND'S FIRST FIREBOAT, THE *GEORGE H. WILLIAMS*, C. 1910. Named after the city's mayor of the day, the *Williams* was built by Ballin and Supple and delivered in 1904. It had a wooden hull and was capable of delivering 6,000 gallons of water per minute. The *Williams* is the first modern fireboat, as department records list a boat for a couple of years during the mid-1880s.

THE *GEORGE H. WILLIAMS*, 1908. The *Williams* is seen here fighting the Crown Shingle Mill fire in 1908. (Gohlston Collection.)

THE *DAVID CAMPBELL*, 1913. The department's second fireboat is seen here on what is presumed to be its maiden voyage. The boat was named for the former chief who was killed at a fire in 1911. Campbell's widow christened the boat in front of 1,500 spectators, and the Fire Department Band was on hand to perform.

THE CAMPBELL UNDER FULL STEAM, 1915. Fireboats demonstrate on the Willamette River for various occasions, but especially when escorting the Rose Festival fleet into harbor. The *Campbell*, built by Ballin and Supple, was 120 feet long, steam driven, and the first steel-hulled fireboat in the department.

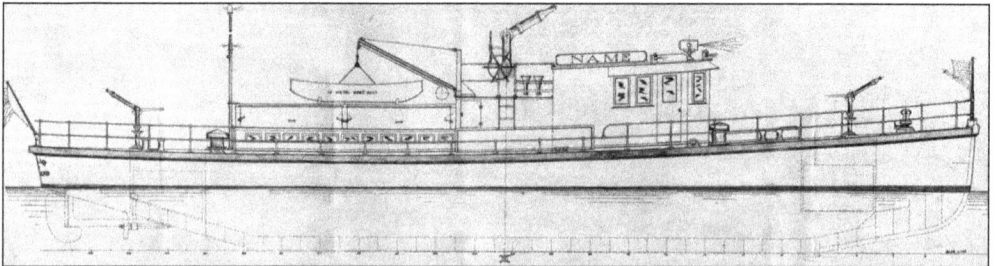

PLANS FOR STEEL FIREBOAT, 1927. A side view of the plan for one of three new identical twin-screw fireboats that were delivered to the fire department in 1927 and 1928. They were built by the Baker Construction Company at a cost of about $100,000 each and were funded by bonds passed in 1926. The hull lengths were 87 feet, and the boats were gasoline powered and could pump 8,000 gallons per minute.

FIREBOAT No. 2 IN ITS SLIP, 1947. The new *David Campbell* was the first one of the three delivered and still serves in a reserve capacity to this day. This *Campbell* replaced the original one, which was decommissioned in 1927.

FIREBOAT No. 3, 1945. The *Karl Gunster* serves as a floating hydrant. Pictured from left to right are Capt. Joseph Allerton, pilot James Copeland, and Wilson Tolson. The *Gunster* was named for Lieutenant Gunster, who was killed in the line of duty in 1921.

TURRET NO. 1, 1950. Also known as a turret wagon, Turret No. 1 was a 1931 Federal. Turrets worked with fireboats, driving to a fire, laying into the boat, and then acting as a turret or as a manifold. Before the wide use of radios, turret drivers would sometimes have a difficult time communicating their position to the boat, especially at night.

FIREBOAT NO. 1 OUTSIDE ITS FLOODED STATION, 1964. The *Mike Laudenklos* was located near the east end of the Hawthorne Bridge. Fireboats assist with harbor duties as well as with fighting fires, and during floods, they are called upon to clear debris that may damage bridges and other structures. The *Laudenklos* was named for the long-serving assistant fire chief who died in 1923. This boat replaced the *Williams*, which was decommissioned upon the arrival of the *Laudenklos*.

74

FIREBOAT No. 1 DEMONSTRATES ON THE WILLAMETTE RIVER, 1966. During the early 1960s, aerial ladders were added to fireboats. Here the *Mike Laudenklos* demonstrates near the Broadway Bridge. In the late 1960s, firefighters William Keys and Everett Bilyeu found a way to pump coloring into the water streams during such displays, something that is still done today.

THE *VIRGIL SPENCER* BEGINS TO SINK, 1972. Purchased to replace the older, slower boats, the jet-driven *Spencer* had a less-than-auspicious beginning, sinking during its maiden voyage. Three holes in the pump casing caused water to flood in, and it sank in two minutes. Here Joe Baron (on boat) and Leonard Brock work to save the boat. The boat was named for Lieutenant Spencer, who died in the line of duty in 1966.

"Well, golly gee, Mrs. McCready, look at the bright side of it: what other fire department has its own submarine?"

A CARTOON POKING FUN AT FIRE COMMISSIONER CONNIE McCREADY, 1972. McCready spent much time and effort bringing the *Spencer* to the department and expected it to become "the pride of the fleet." Before its maiden voyage, the district chief ordered a test run to assure that the department would not look bad if the *Spencer* failed to work well the next day. Years later, a firefighter from Fireboat 2 confessed that during this test run, the boat "made a loud noise and shuddered horribly." It was during this test run that the damage had occurred. Of course, after the shuddering, the man from Boat 2 quickly parked the *Spencer* and told no one, and the rest is history. It was discovered that the jets had sucked in a piece of wood, and the wood had cracked the casing.

THE *VIRGIL SPENCER* AND *KARL GUNSTER* AT FIREBOAT HOUSE NO. 3, C. 1976. Unlike Boathouse Nos. 1 and 2, Fireboat No. 3's house floated and was mobile. In fact, it was located at three sites during its life. Here it is located at Terminal No. 4 in North Portland.

HARBOR PATROL BOATS *KARL PREHN* AND **L. V. *JENKINS*, C. 1978.** In 1973, the department took over the duties of the police bureau's Harbor Patrol and added these boats to its fleet. The *Prehn* was named for a longtime Harbor Patrol officer, and the *Jenkins* was named for a police chief.

DEDICATION CEREMONY FOR THE NEWLY REMODELED DAVID CAMPBELL, 1976. In 1975, the *Campbell* was taken to Coos Bay for a complete refurbishment. The overhaul included conversion to diesel and a redesigned instrument panel and cabin designed by Donald Strech. Pictured from left to right are Vernon Buss, Douglas Young, John Lisoski, and Donald Strech. Buss copyrighted the department's training manual, *Fire Emergencies aboard Cargo Ships in Port*, in 1979 and has a fireboat named for him.

FIREBOAT DAVID CAMPBELL, C. 1976. Here the *Campbell* is marked as Harbor Patrol Boat No. 2. With the addition of the harbor-patrol boats, the department had a seven-boat fleet at its largest point.

Six

LIFE IN PORTLAND FIRE STATIONS

A fire station holds a special place in its community. It has been said that the hardest thing to bring to a neighborhood is a fire station, and the hardest thing to remove from a neighborhood is a fire station. Since the earliest volunteer days, firefighters have taken great pride in their firehouses and the equipment kept inside.

In the volunteer era, the firehouse was best described as a social center for a fraternal organization. Members of status in the community, such as prominent businessmen and city leaders, made up much of the ranks of the early volunteers, thus making service appealing, attracting able-bodied men to the firehouse, and making it a place to be and be seen.

Historically, the buildings were constructed based on the types of equipment to be used and the number of firefighters who would live there. This has changed over time; as the 20th century progressed, community input has also affected the construction and location of stations.

The firehouse is a unique building that contains all the features of a home. Dormitories—or sleeping rooms—kitchens, parking, and work areas for equipment (in the early days this would be horse and wagon and in recent times, fire engines, trucks, and rescues), and areas for relaxation have always been, and remain, regular features of Portland firehouses.

With the inception of the paid fire department, firehouses often became full-time residences for firefighters. If they did not live in the firehouse itself, most firefighters resided on nearby streets or in adjacent homes. This often solidified their connection to the community. This connection remains today, demonstrated by the pride and care each crew takes in their building and the equipment therein.

HOSE-AND-CHEMICAL NO. 1, C. 1909. This station was located at 221 Southwest Second Avenue. Early in the 20th century, paid units were still occupying the original volunteer stations, such as this one that once belonged to Multnomah Engine No. 2. Capt. William Heath is seated on the right of the hose wagon (left).

STATION NO. 5, C. 1911. Located at 3323 Southwest Front Avenue and opened in 1890, this two-story, wood-frame structure is typical of stations built at the end of the 19th century. The apparatus and horses were in the lower story, and the firefighters slept upstairs. Notice the chain across the apparatus bay to keep any wayward horses from escaping.

STATION NO. 18, 1914. Located at 2200 Northeast Twenty-fourth Avenue and opened in 1913, this bungalow station was the first of its kind. The neighbors in the Irvington neighborhood, where the new engine company was to be placed, did not wish to see a typical two-story brick structure erected in their residential area. Luckily for them, Battalion Chief Lee Holden was a budding architect who designed this bungalow station to fit into any neighborhood. A new era was born, and between 1913 and 1928, thirteen bungalow stations were built in all areas of the city. The bungalows had apparatus floors that were lower than the living quarters. This, combined with an attic, allowed for a two-story hose tower that was invisible from the outside. Capt. William Groce sits in the passenger seat, and Lt. Ira Fitzgerald is to his left. The engine seen here is a 1913 American LaFrance.

STATION NO. 20, 1925. Located at 8210 Southeast Thirteenth Avenue, this station was opened in the early 1920s. The bungalows fit into neighborhoods so well that one had a hard time recognizing them as fire stations. In this instance, the crew attached a sign reading "Ye Fire Station Engine 20" to the front porch. The apparatus was parked behind the right section of the building with the driveway leading to it. The double doors, complete with planter boxes, swung open to allow the engine to exit. The station's crew did the landscaping, and many had ponds and rock gardens.

STATION NO. 32, C. 1933. This station was located in the city hall of what was once the separate town of St. Johns and housed the St. Johns Volunteer Department before being staffed by Portland firefighters. This rock garden and miniature railroad were the work of the resident firefighters, who obviously took great pride in their station's landscaping.

STATION NO. 24, 1914. Located at 5340 North Interstate Avenue and opened in 1911, this two-story brick structure is typical of early-20th-century construction. The apparatus and horses were still located on the floor below the sleeping area. Notice the hose-drying tower is taller than the rest of the structure and appears to have doubled as a lookout tower. The second man from the right is Capt. Willis Smith, who began his career as a volunteer in 1895.

CENTRAL STATION UNDER CONSTRUCTION, 1950. Located at 55 Southwest Ash Street, Central was built to house the department's administration as well as multiple apparatus. The construction also included a drill tower for training exercises. Known as Station No. 1 today, Central still serves many of the same functions as it did when it opened in 1951.

STATION NO. 22, 1964. Located at 7205 North Alta Avenue, this station is located in St. Johns. Sometimes firefighters do not have to travel far to find an emergency. In this case, the gentleman seated in the chair seems to have been in reverse when he thought he was in drive.

A "DUCK" AMPHIBIOUS VEHICLE AT STATION NO. 2, 1948. The amphibious vehicles at Station No. 2, located at 510 Northwest Third Avenue, were used for search-and-rescue operations during the flood of 1948. Pictured from left to right are Oswald Forbes, two U.S. Navy personnel, David Gallaher, and James Adair.

HOSE NO. 2 UPSTAIRS LIVING QUARTERS, C. 1900. The fairly opulent and spacious room harkens back to volunteer days, when volunteer houses were as much fraternal social organizations as fire stations. At this time, Hose No. 2 was located in the original station of volunteer company Protection No. 4.

HOSE NO. 2 DOWNSTAIRS LIVING QUARTERS, C. 1905. The downstairs quarters were not as plush as the upstairs, as they was split in half with the other portion dedicated to the apparatus and horses. In this image, Capt. William Kerrigan (closest to the stove) watches some of his crew playing cards.

STATION NO. 10 LIVING QUARTERS, C. 1905. Chief Edward Grenfell said of the earlier days, "We got an evening off one week, a full day off the next." Because firefighters spent most of their time at the station, they had all the amenities of home, including games and music. Notice the phonograph with the cabinet of wax-cylinder recordings on the wall behind it.

STATION NO. 15 LIVING QUARTERS, C. 1910. In this station, there is a phonograph as well as live music and a pool table. Many of the activities and amenities in a station were dictated by the officer in charge.

STATION NO. 17 WATCH DESK, C. 1915. Capt. James Dillane sits at the watch desk as he and his crew pose for a picture. The watch desk is central to every station. In this image, the ticker tape is visible on top of the desk to the captain's right. This tape told the crew where the fire was and which units were to respond.

INTERIOR OF STATION NO. 5, C. 1914. Firefighter Burr McKinley poses with the apparatus and the "horse power" on the apparatus floor. As much as the fire horse is a beloved part of the early lore of fire departments, living with large animals in the same building had drawbacks. Retired battalion chief Samuel Townsend was not a big fan of it and stated, "It was Terrible in the Summertime. All those flies. We had bedsteads with iron frames and used to drape mosquito netting over them to try to get some sleep. Then when the bell would ring, we nearly broke our necks getting all tangled up in that netting." Also, current retired firefighters who worked in stations that once housed horses have commented that on hot days, the smell of horse urine would surface anew. One can imagine what it was like during McKinley's time.

THE INTERIOR LIVING ROOM OF STATION NO. 18, C. 1915. Each bungalow had its own character and decor. Former firefighter Fred Wagner created the tile artwork of the charging horses and steamer. It was removed from the station before it was sold in 1949 and is located in the public entrance of Station No. 1 today.

PREPARING TO BUTCHER A DEER AT STATION NO. 1, 1946. Apparently the apparatus bay was not exclusively for parking equipment. From left to right, Gale Buchanan, Robert Wuerth, Benjamin Steele, Lyle Goode, and Elijah Watson pose with Watson's kill.

RETIREMENT PARTY FOR ROBERT SIMPSON AT STATION NO. 8, 1952. Pension reforms voted in during 1948 required that all department members, other than the chief, retire no later than age 64. Seated from left to right are Robert Simpson, Heine Larsen, Harold Simpson, and William Bloomquist. Standing are William Carr, Joseph Baron, Robert Carver, Harold Morgan, Arthur Kitto, Donald York, William Hipes, Kenneth Leonard, John Dooney, William Phillips, Verne Kelsey, unidentified, Clyde Carter, Keith Kelly, and Curtis Hansen. Carr was the first African American (1952) appointed to the department. Larson was a former firefighter who still lived in the house after retirement. Such arrangements were not uncommon in the days when older houses, built before the three-platoon system went into effect, had plenty of room and extra beds.

BEAR ATTACK AT STATION NO. 13, 1950. While it looks serious, according to firefighter Donald Manthey, this image was posed using a stuffed bear that had once been part of the City Free Museum. Pictured from left to right are Donald Olsen, Harry McKinstry, and Donald McCormick.

INVITATION TO STATION NO. 33, 1941. This is a flyer for an open-house invitation to view the recently completed station in Linnton. Open houses and other events have always cemented the relationship between the department and the surrounding community.

Public Invited

Open House

By

PORTLAND FIRE DEPARTMENT FIRE STATION
11212 NORTHWEST ST. HELENS ROAD

Mon. - 8:00 p.m. - June 16th

Dance to Modern and
Old Fashioned Music

FIRE HOUSE COFFEE
AND REFRESHMENTS
FREE!

A Community Activity Sponsored by Mayor Earl Riley

OPEN HOUSE AT THE NEW STATION NO. 13, 1955. This station is located at 926 Northeast Weidler Street. Chief Edward Grenfell and Fire Commissioner Stanley Earl pose with Engine No. 13 and crew during the opening ceremonies. The crew, from left to right, are Clarence Myers, Rynold Karls, Estues McCauley, and Bruce McConnell. The apparatus is a 1938 Fageol. Edward Grenfell began his career in 1904 and was fire chief from 1928 to 1957. Many generations of Grenfells served in the department, the first starting in 1883 and the most recent retiring in 2002.

OPEN HOUSE AT NEW STATION NO. 14, 1959. This station is located at 1905 Northeast Killingsworth Street. Numerous single-story brick stations, such as this and Station No. 13, were built during the 1950s, and most have been remodeled over the last few years. Pictured from left to right in front of engine are Battalion Chief John Hetrick, Fire Commissioner Earl's assistant John Faust, Chief Harold Simpson, Mayor Terry Schrunk, Commissioner Mark Grayson, and Commissioner Ormond Bean.

INTERIOR DISPLAY AT STATION NO. 14's OPEN HOUSE, 1959. Displays have been and are still common during open houses, although they are not usually as grand as this one. Capt. William Garrett describes some firefighter duties that he experienced while part of a local community: "I've chased cats out of trees, opened houses for women who have lost their keys, [and] rescued kids from bathrooms after they locked themselves in."

Wesley Hodson Keeps Children in Line at Station No. 19, 1959. This image was taken during a Fire Prevention Week event. The department had many prevention-week activities, including a poster contest for children, with the winners receiving a ride to school on a fire engine. The department had an official photographer from the 1930s to 1982, and four people have served in that capacity. This image is one of the more amusing ones taken by Leon Slater.

Cooking at Central, 1956. Paul Meyers (kneeling) and Frank Oliverio are seen here cooking pies. A good cook, especially one who liked the job, was a valued commodity in any station, and other firefighters seldom complained about the cooking lest they get stuck doing it themselves. Shift officers generally established house duties, such as cooking, so each station rotated duties differently.

EXTERIOR UPKEEP AT STATION NO. 23, 1945. Located at 1917 Southeast Seventh Avenue, this station still exists today but is not owned by the department. Firefighters are responsible for much of the upkeep and chores around a station. In this instance, firefighters are using a 1927 Ahrens Fox truck to assist with cleaning and painting. Notice the "double bubble" windshield that was added to the truck by the department's shops. Also, the two houses to the left of the station were known as "firemen's row" because they were once owned by firefighters who worked at the station. In the days prior to the two-platoon system, firefighters could not stray far from the station, and many lived within a block or two—in this case, within a house or two. Former battalion chief Samuel Townsend described the early days when firefighters were on duty "seven days and seven nights straight, then had one day off." He also lamented that "we signed out to go for meals, but had to be in uniform, so we couldn't go in a bar or saloon."

B-Shift Firefighters Cleaning Hose at Station No. 24, 1976. Chores and training keep firefighters busy at the fire station. From left to right, Ronald Wright, Terrence Johnson, and Earl McCormick clean hoses after a fire. In the days of non-synthetic cotton hose, firefighters would return from a fire and hang the hoses to dry in the hose tower to prevent the molding and decay that would occur if they were left wet.

Decorating Truck No. 1 for the Rose Festival Parade, 1946. For most of the 20th century, stations became floral workshops each June, as at least one apparatus from each district was decorated for the Rose Parade. In this image, the crew and helpers are "sticking roses," which means putting floral sticks on the roses so that they could be attached to the float.

LAYING THE FOUNDATION FOR A ROSE FESTIVAL FLOAT, 1947. From left to right, Joe Baron, Charles Rau, and Louis Ross demonstrate how to begin making a float. Firefighters went into local forests to gather moss to use as a foundation for plants and flowers. This was covered with chicken wire, to which flowers and other decorations were then attached. The moss was then kept wet to maintain moisture for the flowers and other plants. Firefighters often canvassed the local neighborhood for roses and other floral donations or "borrowed" them from local parks.

REPAIRING TOYS FOR THE TOY AND JOY PROGRAM, 1961. The Toy and Joy program began in 1914, and different stations specialized in the repair or manufacture of certain types of toys. After 1951, the basement of Central Station was used as a staging area for making sure each needy child received a toy for Christmas. The firefighter on the right is Sam Soter.

WORKING ON DOLL CRADLES AT STATION NO. 7, C. 1965. This station had the equipment to do carpentry work and, at least this year, produced wooden cradles. The work was done during a firefighter's spare time and produced a great number of toys. Pictured from left to right are Frank Bennetti, Aldro Stuck, and Al Bisenius. Toy and Joy still exists today, operating via donations that make Christmas wishes come true.

Seven

LINE OF DUTY DEATHS

Firefighting has always been a dangerous profession. Where fire exists, lives will be at risk, particularly the lives of those fighting the fire. In the early days, Portland was said to be "built to burn," a reference to the predominantly wood construction of the residences and buildings. At times, such as the great fire of 1873, this proved to be true.

This chapter shares the stories of fire personnel who have died in the line of duty while serving the citizens of Portland. Records from the volunteer era beginning in 1851 are incomplete, and the definition of "line of duty" has changed over the years; however, any lives lost while in the line of duty are tragic. This chapter also illustrates the creation of Portland's line-of-duty-death memorial and how memorial services have evolved over the years.

After the death of Chief David Campbell on June 26, 1911, an annual memorial service to honor those killed while in the line of duty began. In 1928, the David Campbell Memorial was dedicated to honor our fallen firefighters in Portland. Several deaths had occurred prior to Chief Campbell and are included on the memorial.

The memorial includes 32 names (at the date of this publication). An additional 14 names are included in this book due to research done in 2006. Evidence discovered in personnel files, obituaries, and annual reports makes a compelling case for the addition of 12 firefighters who are not currently on the memorial. In addition, two firefighters whose deaths were attributed to cancer contracted due to on-the-job exposure are included, redefining the term "line-of-duty death."

The purpose of this chapter is not to define what constitutes a line-of-duty death but to honor those who made the ultimate sacrifice to their chosen profession and put service to the city before self. Their stories serve as reminders of how fragile life can be. Please enjoy the stories of these courageous individuals who bravely and dutifully served the City of Portland.

Labels within image:
FIREMEN MARCHING IN PROCESSION
HEARSE DRAWN BY THREE FIRE HORSES
CHIEF CAMPBELL'S FIRE AUTO
DAVID CAMPBELL DIED JUNE 26 1911
FUNERAL PROCESSION MARCHING UP FOURTH STREET

CHIEF DAVID CAMPBELL'S FUNERAL PROCESSION IN DOWNTOWN PORTLAND, 1911. Campbell's hearse was pulled by his favorite team of horses from Truck No. 1, and his helmet and coat were placed on the seat of his chief's car. The car was driven by his driver, Thomas Gavin, and Campbell's dog Cole rode along on the floorboard where he was accustomed to riding at the chief's feet. Campbell was a well-known and much-beloved figure in Portland, and his funeral is still one of the most well-attended events in the history of the city. Chief Edward Grenfell later described the scene at the fire, which helps explain why Campbell was hailed as a hero: "It's a miracle 20 to 25 others weren't killed in that fire. Chief Campbell was killed trying to get the others out."

100

THE UNION OIL FIRE, 1911. It was during this fire that Campbell was killed. Campbell had entered the building to make sure that everyone was out, as there was a fear of collapse or explosion. Not long after he entered, there was a great explosion, and he was crushed under falling debris.

AN EARLY CAMPBELL MEMORIAL SERVICE, 1914. Shortly after his death, the Campbell Memorial Fund was established to honor the chief and create a memorial for firefighters killed in the line of duty. The fund also created a Campbell medal for bravery. Pictured from left to right are Willis Smith, Lee Holden, unidentified, Jay Stevens, two unidentified men, widow Wiebka Campbell, unidentified, John Carroll, Helen Eilers, and Michael Laudenklos.

Unveiling and Dedication of the

David Campbell Memorial Monument

Washington and Nineteenth Streets
Portland, Oregon

THURSDAY, JUNE 28, 1928, 2:30 O'CLOCK

Under the auspices of the Trustees of the David
Campbell Medal and Memorial Fund and the officials
of the Portland Fire Department

MR. WALTER S. LONG, President of Trustees, Presiding

GUESTS OF HONOR: His Excellency, the Hon. I. L.
Patterson, Governor of the State of Oregon; City
Commissioners Stanhope S. Pier, A. L. Barbur,
John M. Mann; County Commissioners Amedee M.
Smith, Clay S. Morse and Grant Phegley.

PROGRAMME

Overture, "America"
PORTLAND FIRE DEPARTMENT BAND

Invocation—
REV. OSWALD W. TAYLOR

Address—
HON. GEORGE L. BAKER, Mayor of the City of
Portland

Address—
HON. C. A. BIGELOW, Commissioner of Public
Affairs

Song, "The Vacant Chair"—
Police Quartette: W. A. Tyler, Charles B. Lamb,
George N. Johnson and Floyd R. Burtsch.

Address, "Monuments"—
REV. WILLIAM WALLACE YOUNGSON, D. D.

Community Singing, "America"—
Led by TOMMY LUKE

Unveiling of the Monument under the auspices of the
Drill Team of B. P. O. E. No. 142 as Guard of
Honor, led by T. C. Freiberg, leader, and O. G.
Emig, chairman of the Finance Committee, assisted by Captain W. R. Kerrigan, the oldest in point
of service in the Portland Fire Department, and
Hoseman Tom Gavin, the only man thus far to be
awarded a medal by the David Campbell Memorial
and Medal Fund, for many years the Chief's driver, holding that position at the time of his death.

Salutation to the Flag—
COMMISSIONER STANHOPE S. PIER

Song, "The Star Spangled Banner"—
MME. LEAH LEASKA, accompanied by the Portland
Fire Department Band

Address and Placing of Wreath on Memorial—
EDWARD GRENFELL, Chief of the Portland Fire
Department

Song, "The End of a Perfect Day"—
POLICE QUARTETTE

The Benediction—
REV. WILLIAM WALLACE YOUNGSON, D. D.

Trustees of the David Campbell Memorial and
Medal Fund:

WALTER S. LONG, *President* C. A. BIGELOW, *Treasurer*
W. T. PANGLE, *Secretary* H. R. ALBEE
EX-CHIEF L. G. HOLDEN

DEDICATION PROGRAM FOR THE CAMPBELL MEMORIAL MONUMENT, 1928. Funds continued to be raised, and a site was finally selected in the late 1920s for a permanent line-of-duty-death memorial. A service is still held yearly at the monument on June 26, the date of Campbell's death.

CLEANING THE CAMPBELL MEMORIAL, 1948. The crew of Station No. 3 is seen here cleaning the memorial during 1948's Paint-up Clean-up Week. The annual tribute to Portland's fallen firefighters is held at the memorial located at Southwest Nineteenth Avenue and Burnside Street. On the left, Engine No. 3 is a 1938 Fageol, and on the right, Truck No. 3 is a 1928 American LaFrance sporting the Portland double bubble.

CAMPBELL MEMORIAL SERVICE, 1955. For decades after the construction of the Campbell Memorial, services were still held at David Campbell's grave located in Riverview Cemetery. Pictured from left to right are Fire Commissioner Stanley Earl, Rev. George Turney, Chief Edward Grenfell, Assistant Chief Raymond Dunford, Thomas Ramsey, Robert Robinson, and Cecil Holcomb.

Complimentary. ⊙○

Yourself and Ladies are respectfully invited to attend the Ball to be given by the

Veteran Firemen's Association,

OF THE PACIFIC COAST.

on Thanksgiving Eve, November 25th, 1891, at Hibernian Hall, Cor. Washington and Sixth Streets, Portland, Oregon.

James T. Hopkins,
J. M. Patton,
Robt. Holman,
COMMITTEE.

Mr. _____

NOT TRANSFERABLE.

JAMES REED (NO PICTURE), AUGUST 21, 1881. Reed collapsed and died of an apparent heart attack after helping pull a hand-drawn fire engine to a fire on August 16, 1881. His death occurred at the hospital on August 21, 1881. Reed was a volunteer with Protection No. 4, where he also lived. The Veteran Volunteers assisted with expenses for medical, funeral, and burial services, and the annual ball was a yearly fund-raiser for such activities.

FRED WAGNER (NO PICTURE), FEBRUARY 28, 1890. Wagner was fatally injured while testing a new fire engine at the corner of Southwest Seventh Avenue and Salmon Street. He was struck in the head by a nozzle and never regained consciousness. Fires and a fire's destruction have always drawn a crowd. Here spectators view the aftermath of the 1902 Wolf and Zwicker fire.

TOM O'KEEFE (NO PICTURE), AUGUST 21, 1891. O'Keefe was killed while responding to a fire at Sixteenth Avenue and Burnside Street. He fell from the vehicle while rounding a corner and was crushed beneath the wheels. Horse-drawn apparatus were inherently precarious, with steel wheels and firefighters clinging to what they could. Here a crew from Engine No. 7 shows the common riding practice during the era in 1911.

JOHN G. HEWSTON (NO PICTURE), OCTOBER 3, 1892. Hewston was at the scene of a fire in the Kamm Block (Southwest First Avenue and Pine Street) when he was knocked from his ladder by falling timber. He died of a fractured skull. Fires are dangerous in many ways. Here firefighters battle the Standard Oil fire, about 1900.

THOMAS GRENFELL, MARCH 25, 1896. Grenfell's death was attributed to injuries received on a fire call in January 1896. Grenfell assisted in hauling a fire truck up a steep grade. According to reports, he fell, "badly rupturing himself." A few days before his death in March, he met with a similar injury that convinced him to enter the hospital for an operation for a perforated appendix. He died at the hospital.

DAVID CAMPBELL, JUNE 26, 1911. Chief Campbell entered the structure fire at the Union Oil building at Southeast Salmon Avenue and Water Street to alert his crews of an impending building collapse. All others escaped before an explosion occurred that brought a section of the building down. Campbell died when he was crushed by falling debris.

106

WILLIAM HIGDON (NO PICTURE), JUNE 6, 1912. Higdon was driving Engine No. 6 when a sudden lurch threw him beneath the wagon. He was dragged 100 feet before the wagon stopped; Higdon died at the scene. Pictured is the crew of Station No. 6 in front of their station in 1915.

E. Gustafson.

EMIL G. GUSTAFSON, MARCH 16, 1916. Gustafson died when he came in contact with a 10,000-volt power line while working on the fire-alarm telegraph wires at Northwest Twenty-sixth Avenue and Nicolai Street.

FRANCIS H. MCCORMICK (NO PICTURE), AUGUST 15, 1919. McCormick was killed by a fall from a train trestle after being struck with a fire hose while fighting a fire at the Northwest Box Company in southwest Portland. He was serving on Engine No. 1 at the time, pictured here *c.* 1916.

KARL GUNSTER, JUNE 15, 1921. Gunster was suffocated at a fire on the third floor of the May Apartments at Southwest Fourteenth Avenue and Taylor Street. He was found lying on the floor by Peter Clifford, a firefighter with Engine No. 3, who then dragged him to a window.

OSCAR LEHMAN (NO PICTURE), OCTOBER 3, 1921. Lehman died as a result of a skull fracture sustained in a collision between two fire engines at Southwest Fourth Avenue and Jefferson Street. Pictured is the crew of Engine No. 32 modeling a similar engine—a good illustration of how easy it would be to be thrown from it in an accident.

JAMES S. BALDWIN, JUNE 19, 1922. Baldwin was descending the steps to the basement of a home at 387 Yamhill Street when his neck came in contact with a live drop-cord wire across the basement opening. He fell into the water while in contact with the energized wire and was electrocuted. He died at the scene.

OSCAR B. GABRIEL, OCTOBER 25, 1922. Gabriel was killed when a wall fell on him during a fire at Washington High School.

FRED H. RITTENOUR, FEBRUARY 1, 1923. Rittenour died when he fell from a loft in the engine house at Station No. 19, located at 6049 Southeast Stark Street.

ADOLPH W. WEFEL, JUNE 1, 1923. Wefel was killed when a two-story brick chimney fell on him during the overhaul phase of a multi-house fire at North Benton Avenue and Clackamas Street. Lieutenant Wefel (right) and Engineer Ezro Johnson are seen here seated in the engine outside of Station No. 13.

WILLIAM E. WILBUR, APRIL 7, 1926. Wilbur was at a house fire at 848 Northeast Clackamas Street. After climbing down a ladder, he had a seizure, suffered a heart attack, and died.

CHARLES A. RYAN, MAY 20, 1928. Ryan was rehearsing for the Rose Festival Parade Ladder Drill Team at Southwest Taylor Street and Chapman Street when a leather safety belt holding him to firefighter William McCreery broke, causing both men to fall from the ladder to their deaths.

WILLIAM J. McCREERY, MAY 20, 1928. McCreery was rehearsing with Charles Ryan; both men fell to their deaths.

HARRY JOSEPHSON (NO PICTURE), JULY 23, 1928. Josephson died when he lost his balance and fell 25 feet from a power pole at Southeast Fifty-first Avenue and Hawthorne Boulevard. He landed on the pavement and fractured his skull. Josephson died while working on the fire-alarm system. This 1931 image shows the type of fire-alarm telegraph wires he was working on when he fell.

WALTER McBRIDE, DECEMBER 19, 1929. McBride was found unconscious in bed at Station No. 9, located at 900 Southeast Thirty-fifth Avenue, possibly due to a stroke or hemorrhage of the brain. He was taken to the hospital and later pronounced dead.

RICHARD D. LAISNER, JULY 4, 1930. Laisner died of a heart attack while fighting a fire on Southeast Thirty-seventh Avenue.

HENRY KRIMBEL, OCTOBER 23, 1932. Krimbel fell through a skylight at a third-alarm fire on August 16, 1930, at the Councelor Apartments. He suffered spine injuries from the fall. He returned to work for a time but died on October 23, 1932, apparently due to the effects of the prior fall.

114

CLEMENT M. KEMMER, APRIL 21, 1933. Kemmer died of a heart attack while on duty at Station No. 8 at 45 Northeast Russell Street. He was playing handball as part of the physical fitness program.

GUSTAVE A. STEPHAN, JUNE 26, 1933. Stephan (a theater inspector) died of an apparent heart attack at 68 Northeast Stanton Street, where he stopped to rest after having taken ill while on duty.

FRANK L. KEARNEY, JANUARY 7, 1934. Kearney died instantly in a collision between Engine No. 21 and Squad No. 1 at the intersection of Southwest Fourth Avenue and Pine Street, as the firefighters were responding to an emergency at the Holly Dairy at 406 Northwest Fourteenth Avenue. Nine other firefighters were injured in the collision.

HARRY B. MORROW, JULY 1, 1934. Morrow died of an apparent heart attack while fighting an automobile fire at Southeast Seventeenth Avenue and Division Street.

HARRY U. GARDNER (NO PICTURE), JANUARY 19, 1935. Gardner died of an apparent heart attack while fighting a house fire at Northeast Fifty-seventh Avenue and Sandy Boulevard. Pictured is an image of the department's 1938 yearbook page for Station No. 28, where Gardner was working at the time of his death.

WILLIAM D. HEATH, MARCH 18, 1935. Heath had suffered from heart disease for some time. He felt a heart attack come on after having responded to a fire at the Hotel Lindquist a few hours before. His crew heard him suffer the heart attack and went to his aid, but he died soon after at Station No. 22 at 1233 Southwest First Avenue.

FRANK A. PLATT, MARCH 11, 1937. Platt was crushed between Engine No. 10 and a wall while inspecting the engine. The driver mistakenly reversed. He died on the scene at Station No. 10 at 5830 Southwest Kelly Avenue.

HARRY R. HOWARD, DECEMBER 31, 1939. Howard had an apparent heart attack (coronary thrombosis) while on duty at Station No. 36 at 5247 North Lombard Street.

ERNEST W. BILLS, JUNE 3, 1940.
Bills died at a fire at the Portland
Furniture Manufacturing
Company at 5331 Southwest
Macadam Avenue, when his
canister mask failed after he
entered the building. He was
overcome by carbon monoxide
poisoning and died on the scene.

**CARL G. MARKSTROM, JUNE 3,
1940.** Markstrom also died at
the fire at the Portland Furniture
Manufacturing Company after he
entered the building to attempt
a rescue of Earnest W. Bills.
Markstrom suffered the same fate
and died on-scene.

119

PETER P. KUMPF, DECEMBER 5, 1940. Kumpf succumbed to a heart ailment while on duty at Station No. 23 at 1917 Southeast Seventh Avenue and was taken to a local hospital. He died a few hours later. No details on what prompted the heart problem are listed.

JOSEPH F. ALLERTON, OCTOBER 2, 1945. Allerton was commanding the fireboat at the Oregon Shipyard fire on August 30, 1945. He reported sick following the fire and never returned to duty. Allerton died of bronchial pneumonia.

ELMO S. C. BRADFORD, OCTOBER 25, 1945. Bradford may have died of a stroke while fighting a roadside fire at Southwest Broadway Street and Hoffman Avenue. One obituary states that he died of a heart attack while returning from the fire. It is unknown which account of his death is most accurate.

WILLIAM INGLESBY, JULY 19, 1946. Inglesby died while on duty at Station No. 33 at 10803 Northwest Front Avenue. There is no information regarding the cause of death.

GREGORY A. WARNER, DECEMBER 30, 1946. With Station No. 6, Warner responded to a fire at 2401 Northwest Twenty-third Avenue on December 23, 1946. Upon returning to the station, he suffered a heart attack. He died December 30.

MARION STARK, MARCH 31, 1947. Stark was found in bed, dead of a heart attack, at fire Station No. 8 at 45 Northeast Russell Street in the morning of his shift.

ALFRED J. BERG, NOVEMBER 2, 1948. Berg died of an apparent heart attack while fighting a fire in a commercial building at 8950 North Bradford Street.

DANIEL C. SHAW, APRIL 24, 1949. Shaw died of an apparent heart attack while supervising Engine No. 14 at a house fire at 432 Northeast Russell Street. He collapsed while assisting in raising a ladder to the second floor and died on the scene.

VICTOR D. BROWN, DECEMBER 4, 1957. Brown died of acute pneumonia and generalized arteriosclerosis. No information is provided with regard to how his death was related to his job.

JOHN T. METCALF, AUGUST 14, 1960. Metcalf died when Truck No. 7, on which he was riding, collided with a bus at the intersection of Southeast Twelfth Avenue and Hawthorne Boulevard. He was seated next to the driver and thrown from the apparatus to the pavement. In this image, Metcalf (right) is seated with fellow city-handball-league team champions Lewis Hicks (left) and Arnold Gabriel, c. 1950.

Virgil L. Spencer, October 29, 1966. Spencer fell 40 feet from a catwalk at the B. P. Johns Furniture Company fire when flames from a sawdust bin shot up toward him. He never regained consciousness and died at the hospital.

John L. Devaney, February 15, 1977. Devaney died from a heart attack while fighting a fire in a shed at 4000 Southwest Shattuck Road.

JEFFREY S. TUGGLE, APRIL 1, 1993. Tuggle died of cancer that was connected to the cumulative effects of fire byproduct exposure during his career.

STEVEN E. HIGLEY, DECEMBER 30, 2004. Higley was diagnosed with non-Hodgkin's lymphoma in October 2003. This was connected to the cumulative effects of fire byproduct exposure during his career and resulted in his death.

INDEX

www.ingramcontent.com/pod-product-compliance
Lightning Source LLC
Chambersburg PA
CBHW050658150426
42813CB00055B/2219